SEVEN LAKES
LIBRARY

W9-DDE-438

DARK ANGEL

Geoffrey Wansell

Arcade Publishing • New York

PREFACE

The opportunity to return to a subject is a rare privilege for a biographer, and that is why this book means such a great deal to me. Cary Grant is, was, and always will be one of the great movie stars, but when I first came to write a biography about him, fifteen years ago, I don't think I appreciated fully the marvellous subtlety of his talent.

For me, then, Grant was a star we knew and loved, but he was also a man who was somehow always hiding a secret behind the dark, polished sheen of his charm. That was why I first set out to write about him, to see whether I could understand what lay behind his permanently dazzling smile.

My first biography began in a small stuffy flat in Mayfair, when I met the man who always introduced himself by saying, 'Hello, I'm Cary Grant' (even though hardly a man or woman in the world would not have recognized him instantly), and finished in Los Angeles, where I talked to old actors and directors who had worked with him. But looking back, I am not certain that my first portrait did not underestimate the depth of Grant's talent, and the meticulous precision of his acting, by so carefully considering the personal drama that lay behind it. It brought the dark side of his character to life, certainly, but did not quite balance it with proper tribute to his incandescent screen presence.

That is why I was so pleased to be given this opportunity to return to Grant's life, and to write a new, illustrated biography. This time, more than a decade and a half later, I hope I have managed to balance both sides of his life, the pain of his childhood against the pleasure that his particular, exquisite talent has brought to millions. In doing so, I hope I have demonstrated that he was, though troubled, still one of the screen's finest actors.

The journey to refine my thoughts took me back to Los Angeles, and introduced me to many more people who knew and loved Cary Grant. It also took me to libraries and archives in both Britain and the United States, and to seek the help and advice of critics and actors, directors, fellow stars and friends. It is impossible to name them all, but I hope that they will all accept these personal and heartfelt thanks.

But I must thank a handful of people in particular. Juliet Brightmore researched the pictures quite brilliantly, Caroline Taggart did every bit as good a job on the text, and Penny Phillips at Bloomsbury orchestrated the whole process with consummate skill. As ever, my agents Rivers Scott and Gloria Ferris were an unfailing source of support and advice. None, of course, is to blame for my conclusions; those are mine alone. But they each helped me immensely to pay tribute to one of the cinema's authentic stars.

Geoffrey Wansell
1996

FOR MY MOTHER

Copyright © 1996, 2011 by Geoffrey Wansell

All Rights Reserved. No part of this book may be reproduced in any manner without the express written consent of the publisher, except in the case of brief excerpts in critical reviews or articles. All inquiries should be addressed to Arcade Publishing, 307 West 36th Street, 11th Floor, New York, NY 10018.

Arcade Publishing books may be purchased in bulk at special discounts for sales promotion, corporate gifts, fund-raising, or educational purposes. Special editions can also be created to specifications. For details, contact the Special Sales Department, Arcade Publishing, 307 West 36th Street, 11th Floor, New York, NY 10018 or info@skyhorsepublishing.com.

Arcade Publishing® is a registered trademark of Skyhorse Publishing, Inc.®, a Delaware corporation.

Visit our website at www.arcadepub.com.

10 9 8 7 6 5 4 3 2 1

Library of Congress Cataloging-in-Publication Data is available on file.

ISBN: 978-1-61145-310-2

Printed in China

Contents

PROLOGUE 6

CHAPTER ONE
ARCHIE LEACH *12*

CHAPTER TWO
DARK VENUS *22*

CHAPTER THREE
SCREWBALL *46*

CHAPTER FOUR
MR LUCKY? *70*

CHAPTER FIVE
NOTORIOUS *92*

CHAPTER SIX
LONELY HEART *120*

CHAPTER SEVEN
FINAL BOW *148*

CHAPTER EIGHT
JENNIFER AND BARBARA *172*

FILMOGRAPHY *190*
INDEX *191*

PROLOGUE

T

To millions of movie-goers around the world, Cary Grant will forever epitomize the glamour, and the style, of Hollywood in its golden years. With his dark hair and even darker eyes, mischievous smile and effortless elegance, he was, is and always will be indelibly one of the great movie stars. Since his death in 1986, the incandescence of his screen image has not dimmed for a single moment.

In a career spanning four decades, Cary Grant became the man every woman longed for. As Burt Reynolds once put it, 'He was touched by the gods. When he walked into a room you had to look at him. Men liked him as well as women, and that is incredibly rare.' Certainly if the women in his audience were hypnotized, their male partners never for one moment felt threatened. They only wished that they could match his ageless, apparently effortless appeal. The actor and comedian Steve Lawrence summed it up neatly when he said, 'When Cary walked into a room, not only did the women primp, the men straightened their ties.'

'There is a frightening side to Cary that no one can quite put their finger on.'

ALFRED HITCHCOCK

LEFT: STAR IN THE MAKING: GRANT IN MADAME BUTTERFLY IN 1932. ABOVE RIGHT: THE FINISHED ARTICLE, OPPOSITE GRACE KELLY IN TO CATCH A THIEF, MORE THAN TWENTY YEARS LATER.

Yet Cary Grant could, with the arch of an eyebrow or the merest hint of a smile, question his own image. He managed to blend irony and romance in a way that few other stars have ever done, by slyly never appearing to take himself too seriously, and mixing his own unique mixture of naïveté and worldliness. As a result, the veteran critic Charles Champlin believes he was one of the last 'great unconscious prototypes' of the cinema, a star who helped to define wit, charm, refinement and romance. There was, in Champlin's words, 'never anyone quite like him'.

In seventy-two films between 1932 and 1966, Grant meticulously furnished and then burnished his own screen image. He transformed himself from the tall, dark and handsome matinee idol of *Madame Butterfly* in 1932 to the brilliant farceur C.K. Dexter Haven in *The Philadelphia Story* in 1941; only then to refine himself still further, first as the ambiguous, brooding government agent Devlin in *Notorious* in 1946 and then as the enigmatic John Robie in *To Catch a Thief* in 1953.

It was a remarkable achievement, and one which ensured that Grant's unique appeal hardly dimmed in the years after his retirement in 1966. His image shines out from advertising hoardings even now, a decade after his death.

ABOVE: Tall, dark and
handsome: Grant in *The
Toast of New York* in
1937. But there was more
to him than looks, as he
proved with Katharine
Hepburn in *Bringing Up
Baby* (*below right*) and
The Philadelphia Story
(*opposite*).

When *Time Out* magazine in London in
May 1995 asked more than a hundred
leading film directors and producers to
list their favourite movie actor of all
time, Cary Grant came second on their
list, even though he had not appeared in
a new movie for very nearly three
decades. Only Marlon Brando got more
votes. James Stewart, Robert Mitchum,
Robert de Niro, Burt Lancaster, Spencer
Tracy and Humphrey Bogart were all
considered *less* successful film actors
than Cary Grant by a group of directors
and producers as diverse as Pedro
Almadovar, John Milius, Billy Wilder,
Jeremy Thomas, Nik Powell, Stephen
Frears and Fred Zinnemann. And no

fewer than four of Grant's films made it
into their choice of the hundred best
films of all time — *Bringing Up Baby*,
The Philadelphia Story, *Notorious* and
North by Northwest.

Over the years, some of
Hollywood's greatest directors shared
their view. Cary Grant made five films
with Howard Hawks, four with Alfred
Hitchcock (who called him his favourite
leading man), four with Leo McCarey,
three each with Stanley Donen and
George Cukor, not to mention others
with Michael Curtiz, Clifford Odets, Joe
Mankiewicz and Frank Capra. To
Capra, Cary Grant was 'Hollywood's
greatest farceur', while George Cukor
called him 'the greatest exponent of a
very subtle kind of human comedy'.

The great directors, like the audiences, recognized Grant's delicate
subtlety as an actor. His was an insolent
charm, once seen never forgotten. And
he carefully sustained his performance

off the screen as well as on, maintaining
his image as the suave, romantic leading
man in his private life every bit as deter-
minedly as he did in his films.

As the critic Pauline Kael once said,
'Everyone likes the idea of Cary Grant.
Everyone thinks of him affectionately,
because he embodies what seems a
happier time, a time when we had a
simpler relationship to a performer.
We could admire him for his timing and
his nonchalance.... He appeared before
us in radiantly shallow perfection and
that was all we wanted.... We didn't
want depth from him, we asked only
that he be handsome and silky and make
us laugh.'

Yet though we seemed to know him
so well, somehow Cary Grant also
remained eternally elusive, always able
to make his escape. In 1934 Mae West
was asking him to 'Come up sometime
and see me' in *She Done Him Wrong*,
while thirty years later Audrey Hepburn

THE DARK AND MENACING
SIDE TO GRANT THAT ALFRED
HITCHCOCK CAPTURED IN
NOTORIOUS IN 1946.

was doing the same thing in *Charade*: 'Won't you come in for a minute? I don't bite, you know, unless it's called for.' But neither leading lady ever quite managed to capture him. Even the magnificent Marlene Dietrich did not land him in *Blonde Venus*, and neither did Marilyn Monroe in *Monkey Business*.

For me, it was this elusive quality that came to fascinate three generations of film makers and filmgoers. The disarming smile was always in place, as was the mannered charm, but somehow there

was always something going on behind it, something that defied description; something dangerous, even slightly threatening. As Alfred Hitchcock once put it, 'There is a frightening side to Cary that no one can quite put their finger on.'

It was this darker, more mysterious side that Hitchcock himself drew out of Grant in four films, most spectacularly in *Notorious*. But it did nothing to detract from his enormous appeal to audiences in material of all kinds, especially romantic comedy. The director Peter Bogdanovich calls him 'the ideal leading man, the perfect zany, the admirable dandy and the most charming rogue'. But Cary Grant also turned down, or

sidestepped, some of the most important roles in the cinema in the quarter of a century between 1940 and 1965. He wanted to play James Stewart's role in Capra's *It's a Wonderful Life*, and Monty Woolley's in *The Man Who Came to Dinner*, but in the end decided against them both. He was offered Bogart's part in Billy Wilder's *Sabrina*, Gregory Peck's in *Beloved Infidel*, Ronald Colman's in *A Double Life*, Gary Cooper's in *Love in the Afternoon* and James Stewart's in Hitchcock's *Rope*, but turned them all down. He declined David Niven's role in *Around the World in Eighty Days* and James Mason's in Cukor's *A Star Is Born*, just as he turned down Mason's role in Stanley Kubrick's *Lolita* and William Holden's in *The Bridge on the River Kwai*. He refused to play Professor Higgins in *My Fair Lady*, and insisted that Robert Preston, not he, should play *The Music Man*.

Had he played even half of these roles, there would be few who would deny that he was, in the words of the critic Richard Schickel, 'not merely the greatest movie star of his era but the medium's subtlest and slyest actor as well'. But his determination never to abandon the security of playing the character he had so carefully created for the screen made him unwilling to experiment or to display his extraordinary talent as a film actor in unexpected roles.

For no matter how debonair Grant may have appeared, both on the screen and off it, there was a darker side to his character that he took pains never to allow to surface in public. Almost the only occasions when it did so were when his first four wives sued him for divorce, and then he had no control over events. But if there were fears and insecurities hidden behind that ageless, self-deprecating smile, Grant took care to hide them.

Though he experimented with psychoanalysis, and took the hallucinogenic drug LSD on more than a hundred occasions during therapy sessions in the 1960s, he would always introduce himself to a stranger by saying, 'Hello, I'm Cary Grant', even though his was one of the best known faces in the world. He saw himself as a product, a personality that had been tested in the marketplace and should never be allowed to display its weaknesses. His was a mask behind which he preferred to remain, and it is one reason why he refused an offer of $5 million to write his life story: to see him on the screen was enough. That was where Cary Grant came to life.

Grant managed to conceal the contradictions in his personality with the same steely professionalism that he brought to his screen performances. No matter how many times he may have fussed on the set, dithered over details of his deals, refused to spend money needlessly, tried to avoid autograph hunters, declined to appear on television, claimed to be nervous in public and insisted that he was 'a bum' at home, not one single member of his audience every truly believed him. To millions of his fans around the world he was forever the fairy-tale hero, the king of hearts, one of the handful of stars who could make the world seem a more glamorous and romantic place.

As the American writer Tom Wolfe put it, 'To women he is Hollywood's lone example of the Sexy Gentleman. And to men and women, he is Hollywood's lone example of a figure that America, like most of the West, has needed all along: a Romantic Bourgeois Hero.' The fact that he was born into a working-class family in Bristol, the lonely child of a poor trouser presser, can never detract for one moment from Cary Grant's place as one of the icons of the modern cinema: Hollywood's dark angel.

'AW... YOU CAN BE HAD.' TWO OF THE MANY WOMEN WHO SET THEIR SIGHTS ON GRANT ON THE SCREEN: MAE WEST IN THE CLASSIC *SHE DONE HIM WRONG* IN 1933 (*TOP*), AND AUDREY HEPBURN IN *CHARADE* EXACTLY THIRTY YEARS LATER (*ABOVE*). THE FAMOUS CROP-DUSTER IN *NORTH BY NORTHWEST* IN 1959 (*LEFT*) CAME CLOSER THAN EITHER.

CHAPTER ONE • ARCHIE LEACH

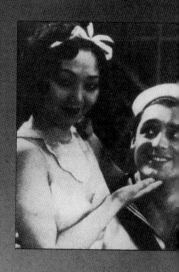

It could hardly have been a less likely beginning. Cary Grant, the man destined to become the cinema's 'fairy-tale hero', was born Archibald Alec Leach, the only child of a poor tailor's presser and an obsessed, doting mother, in a small terraced house on the outskirts of Bristol just four years after the turn of the century. But his birthplace and his childhood were to leave an indelible mark on the actor Marlene Dietrich called 'Hollywood's only true prince'.

The boy born Archie Leach never lost a fondness for his real name or the town of his birth. When he first settled in Hollywood in 1932, he called his new Sealyham terrier Archie Leach. And in film after film, from *Gunga Din* to *His Girl Friday* and *Arsenic and Old Lace*, Cary Grant made jokes about a miserable chap called Archie Leach.

Archie Leach's parents were Victorians. His mother, Elsie Kingdon, was the daughter of a shipwright. She did not care for alcohol or tobacco, and certainly did not believe in spoiling the child, especially not her own. With dark eyes and a dark olive skin, which she passed on to her son, this thin, wiry

woman had a waspish temper. By contrast, Archie's father, Elias Leach, was the raffish son of a potter, and there was always a twinkle in his eye. The mustachioed Elias Leach married Elsie Kingdon in May 1898. He was twenty-five, she barely twenty-one.

The new Mrs Leach had been married only a few weeks when she realized she was pregnant. She began to prepare for motherhood with the studied precision that she was to bring to the rest of her life. For his part, Elias Leach pressed as many trousers, coats and waistcoats as he could manage at Todd's Clothing Factory in Bristol, determined to provide as best he could for his new family. Their first child, a boy whom they christened John William Elias, was born on 9 February 1899.

But John Leach was a sickly child. Throughout the first year of his life he suffered from regular bouts of fever, and his mother worried herself into illness. She would spend night after night sitting beside his cot, willing him to catch his breath as he struggled against the fever. Then in January 1900, a door was accidentally slammed on John's thumbnail while he was in his mother's arms, and within a week gangrene had developed. Once again a distraught Elsie Leach stayed up to watch over him, until, finally, two days before her son's

'I became an actor for the usual reason – a great need to be liked and admired.'

BEFORE HOLLYWOOD: GRANT AS A STAR IN LIGHT OPERA ON BROADWAY WHEN HE MADE HIS FIRST SCREEN APPEARANCE IN THE SHORT *SINGAPORE SUE* IN 1931.

THE LONELY BOY FROM
BRISTOL: ARCHIBALD ALEC
LEACH, BORN ON
18 JANUARY 1904.

first birthday, the local doctor told her firmly that she had to rest. That night she put her son into his cot and reluctantly retired to her own bed. Young John never woke up.

The conviction that her first son's death had somehow been her fault was never to leave Elsie Leach. The suspicion that she was blighted remained with her for the rest of her life, and she hoarded his memory within her, just as she hoarded his clothes in the bottom drawer of the chest of drawers in her bedroom. By the time she and Elias had moved into a new house in Hughenden Road in Bristol in 1901, she had become the embodiment of Victorian womanhood, turned to stone by grief and a sense of duty. Nevertheless, Elsie Leach was determined that she should bear another child.

It was not until the late spring of 1903, shortly after her twenty-sixth birthday, that she became pregnant again. Her husband was pleased enough, but he felt a little detached from the fierce, chill young woman with whom he now shared a meticulously tidy house.

Shortly after one o'clock in the morning of 18 January 1904, with the rain beating against the windows, Elsie Leach gave birth to her second son in the front bedroom of that tiny terraced house in Hughenden Road. The baby had her huge, dark brown eyes and olive complexion, and his father's grin, and she decided to christen him Archibald Alec. He was became the sole reason for her life. There were to be no more children.

As the black-haired baby grew into a sloe-eyed little boy, Elsie Leach's fascination with her son deepened into an obsession. She never wanted his childhood to end. Archie Leach was kept in baby dresses, with his hair in ringlets around his shoulders, long after he had grown out of the black upright pram in which his mother so solemnly wheeled him out most afternoons.

'My mother was not a happy woman,' Cary Grant remembered sadly years later, 'and I was not a happy child because my mother tried to smother me with care. She was so scared something would happen to me.' The prim-faced young woman wanted a dependent being, a child unable to exist without her love and attention. It was an attitude that was first to annoy and then to horrify his father. 'She and my father fought about me constantly,' Grant was to explain. 'He wanted her to let go. She couldn't. I never spent a happy moment with them under the same roof.'

The intensity of his mother's love was to haunt Cary Grant for the rest of his life. Nothing could quench Elsie Leach's ambitions for her son. By the time Archie was four, she had already started to teach him to dance and sing, and she was about to arrange for him to have piano lessons. He was not to be condemned to life in the back streets of Bristol as she was. Each afternoon she would take him for walks through the city's finest Georgian streets to prove there was a life beyond Hughenden Road. In her mind, he was just as entitled to be a 'little gentleman' as the sons of the solicitors and merchants who lived there. The walks were an experience he was never to forget, for they fuelled his dream of affluence and of achieving the success that his mother so dearly wanted for him.

Elsie Leach also impressed on her son that money 'didn't grow on trees' and that he must look after his clothes 'because they're not made of iron'. When he stood in the hall before their afternoon walk, she would straighten the folds of his coat and smooth his long hair. He was her little prince, apart from the world. It was a feeling that he loved. Not that he was not capable of defying her. 'He can be the very devil with his temper,' she would confess from time to time, patting him on the head as she spoke.

Elias Leach, in contrast, sometimes frightened his son. He would take him out into the garden and push him so high on a swing that he had constructed for him that Archie was terrified. His father wanted him to be 'a real boy', the kind who got into trouble and got his knees dirty. But no matter how hard he tried he could not make that happen. His wife was too powerful a personality. The garden swing made no difference. It served only to make Archie forever frightened of heights.

Finally, at the age of four and three-quarters, Archie, whose right shoulder had developed slightly lower than his left and who had also become left-handed (rather to his mother's dismay, for she disapproved of left-handed people), escaped the smocks and girlish dresses of his early years. He found himself instead in dark tweed shorts with thick woollen socks up to his knees. The law demanded that every boy should attend school from the age of five, but Elsie wanted her son to be there sooner.

'Very gradually, I grew accustomed to associating with other children,' Cary Grant was to remember, 'or rather, mostly with other boys. Little boys.' He was asked to be the goalkeeper in the playground football matches at the Bishop Road elementary school — largely because no one else wanted the responsibility. That memory, too, was to remain with him for the rest of his life. 'If the ball slammed past me, I alone — no other member of the team, but I alone — was held responsible for the catastrophe.'

The experience may have been terrifying, but it also made him appreciate applause. 'Right then and there I learned the deep satisfaction derived from receiving the adulation of my fellow little men. Perhaps it began the process that resulted in my search for it ever since. No money, no material reward is comparable to the praise, the shouts

of well done, and accompanying pat on the back of one's fellow man.'

His mother disapproved. She did not want her son getting dirty playing football. If he spilled even a morsel of his food on the starched white tablecloth she laid for lunch on Sunday, she would fine him twopence from the six he received as weekly pocket money, and there were other penalties for untidiness. It meant that young Archie hardly ever received any pocket money at all. For the rest of his life Cary Grant would refuse to eat at a dining table if he could avoid it, just as he would keep his houses meticulously clean and tidy.

There were some diversions. His father took him to Bristol's new Metropole Cinema to see silent serials like *The Clutching Hand*, where the audience stamped and hissed as the villain terrified its heroine, Pearl White. 'We loved each adventure,' he remembered, 'and each following week I neglected a lot of school homework conjecturing how the hero and heroine could possible get out of the extraordinary fix in which they'd been left.' Archie Leach was hooked. He took to going to the new Pringles Picture Palace on Saturdays. 'The unrestrained wriggling and lung exercise of those matinees, free from parental supervision, was the high point of my week.'

The cinema was a haven from the tensions of home, tensions that his father too had been feeling. Finally, in the summer of 1912, Elias Leach announced that he had been offered a better job eighty miles away in Southampton, making khaki army uniforms, and that he had decided to take it. What he did

GRANT'S MOTHER, ELSIE LEACH, WHO DISAPPEARED FROM HIS LIFE FOR TWENTY YEARS WHEN HE WAS TEN.

not tell his wife was that he had also found another woman. In the years to come Cary Grant would hardly remember his father's departure, which had happened when Archie was eight years old. He said only, 'Perhaps I felt guilty at being secretly pleased. Now I had my mother to myself.'

Elias Leach's bid for freedom failed. The cost of two houses and two lives proved too great, and within nine months he was forced to back to Bristol. But her husband's return did nothing to brighten Elsie Leach's demeanour. Quite the opposite: she became steadily stranger. She took to locking every door in the house and asking no one in particular, 'Where are my dancing shoes?' She also washed her hands repeatedly, brushing them every time with a stiff-bristled brush. Though her son did not realize it, the fragile balance of

BROADWAY'S 'PLEASANT NEW
JUVENILE': ARCHIE LEACH IN
THE MUSICAL *GOLDEN DAWN*
IN 1927.

his mother's mind was beginning to fail.

In the early spring of 1914, Elias Leach privately consulted the family's doctor and the local magistrates about his wife's state of mind. Then, in May, without telling his son, he committed her to the local mental hospital at Fishponds. He simply told his only child that his mother had 'gone away for a rest'. Though he would sometimes imply she had sent him a message, Elias Leach would never say whether Elsie would ever come back. He never explained to his ten-year-old son why his mother had disappeared.

As Cary Grant put it bleakly many years later, 'I was not to see my mother again for more than twenty years. By which time my name was changed and I was a full-grown man living in America, thousands of miles away in California. I was known to most people in the world by sight and by name, yet not to my mother.'

The pain of his mother's disappearance drove the young Archie Leach deeper into himself. He took to wandering through the streets of Bristol alone, sitting for hours at the town's quayside watching the ships ease their way out into the Bristol Channel on the evening tide. He would walk home in the gathering dusk, a boy who no longer knew where he belonged, or what was home.

Without his mother's influence, he first became a scruffy boy — whose scout troop once forcibly washed his neck after its dirtiness had lost them a competition — and then suddenly developed an obsession with cleanliness. 'I washed myself constantly, a habit I carried far into adulthood in a belief that if I scrubbed hard enough outside I might cleanse myself inside: perhaps of an imagined guilt that I was in some way responsible for my parents' separation.'

The outbreak of war in August 1914 brought hard times. There was less work at the clothing factory, and Elias Leach was forced to move into his mother's house in Picton Street, Bristol, near the city centre. 'He was a dear, sweet man,' his son remembered, 'and I learned a lot from him. He first put into my mind the idea of buying one good superior suit rather than a number of inferior ones. Then, even when it was threadbare, at least people will know at once it was good.' But Archie Leach stayed out of his father's and his grandmother's way at Picton Street. He started to look after himself, scrounging around in the kitchen looking for food whenever he was hungry, another habit that he was never to lose.

In the first months of 1915 he won a place at the Fairfield Secondary School, not far from his new home. But within a year school had become an irrelevance. He hated mathematics and Latin, although he did not mind geography — 'because I wanted to travel'. Archie

Leach had become a secretive boy with a rebellious streak. If he was caught doing something naughty he would open his dark eyes and raise a single eyebrow in a quizzical style the world would one day come to recognize. And when another boy knocked him over in the playground, snapping one of his front teeth in half, he himself paid out of his pocket money for the remaining piece to be pulled out; for weeks afterwards he kept his mouth closed while the gap closed. By doing so, he perfected the tight-lipped smile that was to become one of his hallmarks on the screen.

As the war dragged on in France, Archie Leach grew taller and further apart from his father. He still roamed the wharves and docks of Bristol, once applying for a job as a cabin boy only to be turned down 'because I couldn't bring permission from my parents'. Then, on a Saturday afternoon in the autumn of 1917, a part-time teacher at Fairfield School, who had been helping to install the new lighting switchboard at the Hippodrome, Bristol's largest theatre, invited him to go backstage with him. The experience changed young Archie's life forever.

'I suddenly found myself inarticulate in a dazzling land of smiling, jostling people wearing and not wearing all sorts of costumes and doing all sorts of clever things,' he remembered later. 'That's when I *knew*. What other life could there *be* but that of an actor?' The lonely thirteen-year-old wanted to become one at once, and took to hanging around the Hippodrome at every opportunity. Then he was introduced to the manager of another of the city's theatres, the Empire, where he was asked to help to move the new arc-lights and change the coloured carbon filters. Archie Leach was hooked.

Before long he had become a part-time call-boy at the Hippodrome, and it was there in the last months of 1917 that he asked one of the performers, the stocky comedian Bob Pender, whether he could have a job as one of the boys in Pender's silent troupe of 'Knockabout Comedians'. Pender was tempted. Some of his boys were about to be called up to fight in Flanders, and he was looking for replacements. He told the stage-struck call-boy that he might consider it — 'providing your parents approve'.

As he ran out of the theatre, the only thing a delighted Archie Leach neglected to tell Pender was that he was not yet quite old enough to leave school. Instead he rushed home and wrote a letter 'purportedly from my own father' giving him permission to join the troupe. Within ten days Pender had written back, inviting him to Norwich, where the troupe was performing, and enclosing the train fare. Archie did not hesitate. Just before six the following morning, he let himself quietly out of his grandmother's house and set off for Norwich. And when he arrived at the Theatre Royal, 'They gave me a short, handwritten contract stipulating that I was to receive my keep and ten shillings pocket money a week.' That day Archie Leach began his career in show-business — by learning how to be an acrobat, another art he was never to forget.

Though Elias Leach was to reclaim his son a few days later, and take him back to school in Bristol, Archie's future

had been settled. In March 1918, two months after his fourteenth birthday, and after making sure that he was expelled from school for inattention and irresponsible behaviour, he was back with Pender's Knockabout Comedians, as a permanent member of the troupe.

'Touring the English provinces with the troupe,' he recalled long afterwards, 'I grew to appreciate the fine art of pantomime. No dialogue was used in our act and each day, on a bare stage, we learned not only dancing, tumbling and stilt-walking, but also how to convey a mood or a meaning without words. How to establish communication silently with an audience, using the minimum of movement and expression; how best immediately and effectively to effect an emotional response — a laugh or, sometimes, a tear.'

Night after night he would stand in the wings after the troupe's act was

finished and watch the show's other performers: 'To respect the diligence it took to acquire such expert timing and unaffected confidence.' Archie Leach took the lessons to heart. 'I strove to make everything I did at least appear relaxed. Perhaps by relaxing outwardly I thought I could eventually relax inwardly; sometimes I even began to enjoy myself on stage.'

The process worked. Archie Leach became one of the eight boys Pender chose to take with him to Broadway in July 1920. In New York, the Pender troupe joined a new revue, *Good Times*, at the huge Hippodrome on Sixth Avenue. They played 'the Hipp' for the next nine months, doing twelve shows a week, including matinees every day

HIS FIRST FILM ROLE, AS AN AMERICAN SAILOR OPPOSITE ANNA CHANG IN *SINGAPORE SUE*.

BROADWAY'S LATEST
LEADING MAN: ARCHIE
LEACH IN 1931.

except Sunday. When they weren't at the theatre, the boys lived with the Penders in an apartment near Eighth Avenue, taking it in turns to cook, wash the dishes and make the beds. In his spare time, Archie Leach would ride up and down Fifth Avenue on the open-air buses, drinking in Manhattan as it drank in the first years of the Roaring Twenties.

When *Good Times* closed, the Pender troupe moved on to B.F. Keith's vaudeville circuit, playing theatres from Cleveland to Milwaukee, and in July 1922 the eight young members of the Knockabout Comedians appeared at the Palace Theatre on Broadway, the pinnacle of vaudeville. Archie Leach was just eighteen.

Now six feet one inch tall and with a distinctive cleft chin, Archie Leach decided to strike out on his own. He

took a room in Greenwich Village and tried to find work as a solo performer. The only problem was that there were very few jobs on offer in vaudeville that summer. So, to supplement his income, he sold ties from a suitcase on Broadway. He had befriended the Australian-born artist and designer Jack Kelly, later to become the costume designer Orry-Kelly. Kelly would buy ties for a dollar each, paint them and then give them to Archie to sell for three dollars. They shared the profits.

One evening in the late summer of 1922, Archie Leach found himself at a dinner party sitting beside George Tilyou, the owner of the Steeplechase Park racecourse on Coney Island. When Tilyou heard that Archie could walk on stilts, he suggested that he could advertise his new track by walking through the crowds at Coney Island on stilts. Archie was in no position to refuse. He needed the money.

Within a week he was on top of six-foot stilts, wearing a sandwich-board and dressed in a bright green coat with long black trousers, being jostled by the milling New Yorkers on Coney Island. His pay was three dollars every weekday and five dollars on Saturday and Sunday, but he soon drew such large crowds that his salary was doubled. Shortly afterwards he began supplementing even that with free hot dogs for standing beside one of the island's hot-dog stands. 'Then I fixed up a deal with a restaurant and an ice cream palace, and I got all the food I wanted free.'

Archie Leach was to put the experience to good use. A few weeks later he and Bob Pender's son Tommy were

offered a booking back at the Hippodrome in a show called *Better Times*. They decided to call themselves the Walking Stanleys, not least because part of the act was to be done on stilts. When *Better Times* closed, Pender and Archie moved on to Alexander Pantages's circuit on the west coast of the United States, and in the first months of 1924, at the age of twenty, Archie got his first glimpse of the city that was to become his home. He arrived in Los Angeles as one of the Walking Stanleys. 'I saw palm trees for the first time in my life, and I was impressed by Hollywood's wide boulevards and their extraordinary cleanliness in the pre-smog sunshine,' he was to recall later. 'I didn't know I would make my home there one day. And yet I did know....'

One thing Archie Leach certainly knew was that in 1924 performers who talked were usually paid more than silent comedians. And if he wanted to become an actor he would have to start talking on the stage. The only difficulty was his voice. He thought he sounded like an Australian, and so did his friends — so much so that they took to calling him 'Kangaroo' and 'Boomerang'. Orry-Kelly remembers him as 'having a rather thick English accent, though he was losing it fast'. After struggling and failing to make himself understood, Archie Leach accepted the inevitable. He could not alter the sound of his voice overnight. It was going to be some time before he could become an actor. He settled instead for being a straight man to stand-up comedians. And in the next five years, he played almost every small town in America. 'I learned to time laughs.

When to talk into an audience's laughter. When not to wait for a laugh. In all sorts of theatres, of all sizes, playing to all sorts of people, timing laughs that changed at every single performance.'

And he never stopped standing in the wings watching vaudeville's great straight men, like George Burns. Years later Cary Grant acknowledged that he took his style as a comedian from Burns. 'The straight man says the plant line, and the comic answers it. He doesn't move while that line is said. That's the comedy line. The laugh goes up and up in volume and cascades down. As soon as it's getting a little quiet, the straight man talks into it, and the comic answers it. And up goes the laugh again.... George was an absolute genius, timing his laughs with that cigar.'

In 1925 and 1926, Archie Leach painstakingly worked on his accent, slowly transforming it into the distinctive mixture of Cockney and upper-class English, tinged with what seemed like mock Australian, that would eventually become his hallmark. And as his accent and timing improved on the stage, so his confidence grew off it. It gave him the courage to turn himself into a musical-comedy star. In the summer of 1927, it was no handicap to sound English in musical comedy. Jack Buchanan had taken Broadway by storm the year before in André Charlot's *London Revue of 1924*, and Archie sensed that if he could emulate the clipped English tones and apparently nonchalant style of Buchanan — which Noël Coward was also using to great effect on Broadway in his own play *The Vortex* — he would have a chance of success. As Grant

himself put it, 'Archie Leach, the drop-out runaway from Bristol, studied men like Jack Buchanan and Noël Coward, and became Cary Grant.'

A friend introduced him to the stage director Reggie Hammerstein, whose elder brother Oscar was the lyricist of Sigmund Romberg's hit *The Desert Song* and whose uncle Arthur was one of Broadway's greatest impresarios. Reggie Hammerstein urged the twenty-three-year-old Archie Leach to take more voice lessons as well as singing lessons, and shortly afterwards took him to meet his uncle, who was about to stage a new operetta called *Golden Dawn*, with lyrics by his nephew. The story was hackneyed, but there was a good part for a handsome young juvenile. Hammerstein offered him a contract at $75 a week for 'the rest of the 1927/28 season'. The impresario also kept an option to renew for a further five years, guaranteeing a weekly salary of $100 in 1928/29, rising to $800 in 1932/33.

In October 1927 *Golden Dawn*, with Archie Leach as the juvenile lead and Louise Hunter as the star, duly went on tour before Broadway. When it opened in New York on 30 November the critics were cool. Almost the only thing they liked was the 'pleasant new juvenile', the 'competent young newcomer' Archie Leach. In spite of

the reviews, however, the name of Hammerstein was enough to sustain it for five months and 184 performances.

Immediately after the closure of *Golden Dawn*, Hammerstein offered his new juvenile lead a better part — that of the young man in *Polly*, a musical version of the comedy *Polly with a Past*. It was the part Noël Coward had played in London. No sooner had rehearsals begun, however, than Archie Leach started to fret. His clothes weren't quite right, his lines didn't work, he couldn't make the audience laugh. He niggled and fussed, fretted and complained

HOLLYWOOD HOPEFUL: EXACTLY WHAT THE STUDIO WAS LOOKING FOR.

'ONLY ONE THING. YOU'LL NEED TO CHANGE YOUR NAME.' ARCHIE LEACH BECOMES CARY GRANT AND CHAINS HIMSELF TO PARAMOUNT IN 1932.

for six weeks until finally he was dropped from the cast before *Polly* even reached Broadway.

Archie Leach's good looks saved him. Marilyn Miller, the musical comedy star, chose him to replace her leading man in *Rosalie*, and Arthur Hammerstein's arch-rival, Florenz Ziegfeld, the show's producer, asked the impresario if he would release him. Hammerstein flatly refused, and retaliated by selling Archie's contract to the brothers Lee and J.J. Shubert, Broadway's biggest theatrical producers. Within weeks the Shuberts had cast him as the villain in *Boom, Boom*, a new musical starring Jeanette MacDonald.

'The heavy in our show,' MacDonald remembered later, 'was a dark-eyed, cleft-chinned young Englishman who, in spite of his unmistakable accent, was cast as a Spaniard.... He was absolutely terrible in the role, but everyone liked him. He had charm.' Archie's charm did not save *Boom, Boom*, which closed after seventy performances, but it did bring him and his leading lady one benefit. They were invited for a screen test together by Paramount Publix Pictures at their Astoria studios in New York.

Movies were news. The talkies had just happened, and Metro-Goldwyn-Mayer's *Broadway Melody* had caused a sensation. A screen test was an opportunity no young actor wanted to miss, a first step on the ladder that could lead to Hollywood. But Archie Leach was destined to miss it. Paramount loved Jeanette MacDonald and asked her to go to California at once to make *The Love Parade*, opposite Maurice Chevalier, but they told Archie Leach that his neck was 'too thick' and his legs were 'too bowed'.

To console himself he went out and bought a 1927 Packard sport phaeton. It was the first car he had ever owned. The Shuberts, determined not to pay him for sitting around doing nothing, quickly put him into another musical, *A Wonderful Night*, a new version of Johann Strauss's opera *Die Fledermaus*, but the show opened two days after the great Wall Street Crash of October 1929, and New York's theatre-goers had other things on their mind. It closed after 125 performances.

Sporting a new raccoon coat and living in an apartment in Greenwich Village with three friends, Archie Leach should have been a young man about town. He was twenty-five, dazzlingly handsome, fairly comfortably off and distinctly eligible. But, somehow, he never seemed at ease with women. As he was to admit later, 'That was my trouble. Always trying to impress someone. Now wouldn't you think that with a new, shiny, expensive, open car, an open-neck shirt, with a pipe in my mouth to create a carefully composed study of nonchalance, sportiveness, savoir-faire and sophistication, I would cut quite a swathe amongst the ladies? Nothing of the sort. In all those years in the theatre, on the road and in New York, surrounded by all sorts of attractive girls, I never seemed able to fully communicate with them.'

Undeterred by the fate of *A Wonderful Night*, the Shuberts put him into the touring version of the musical *The Street Singer*, opposite Queenie Smith. Archie Leach found himself spending the winter of 1930 crossing provincial America watching the unemployment lines grow longer. In the afternoons he would take long bus rides, or drive off into the countryside by himself. When *The Street Singer* came to the end of its tour in the spring of 1931, the Shuberts immediately offered him the summer in St Louis, where they were responsible for programming the open-air Municipal Opera. Rather than relinquish $400 a week, most of which he had been saving carefully, he accepted. But the depression was beginning to bite, and the summer season had hardly begun when the Shuberts asked everyone in the company to take a pay cut. Everyone agreed to do so — except Archie Leach. Even at this early stage of his career, he was unwilling to accept the idea that his value could be cut. The Shuberts duly fired him when the season came to an end.

But St Louis brought Archie Leach one benefit. A glowing piece in *Variety* had caught the eye of the impresario William Friedlander, who was looking for a handsome young juvenile to play the romantic lead in his new musical, *Nikki*. Friedlander sent a man to St Louis to see the 'new young juvenile', liked what he heard and offered him the part of Cary Lockwood. Archie Leach gratefully accepted. A story about young airmen in Paris after the First World War, written by John Monk Saunders, who was married to the show's star, Fay Wray, *Nikki* opened in New York on 29 September 1931. But even the musical theatre was not immune to the depression that was starting to grip America. *Nikki* closed after just thirty-nine performances.

Now, ironically, Archie Leach was offered a film role at the Paramount Publix studios at Astoria. The thick neck and bow legs that had been such a handicap two years before did not seem to matter any more, and he was paid $150 for six days' work, playing an American sailor in a short to be called *Singapore Sue*. He enjoyed the experience and began to wonder whether perhaps the movies might be the only part of the entertainment business that would be 'recession proof'. Fay Wray, who was already packing for Hollywood to play the lead in *King Kong*, urged him to follow her and take a chance. And Billy Grady of the William Morris Agency also encouraged him to think about the movies: 'You must become a leading man. Why don't you go to California?'

Finally, in early November 1931, Archie Leach took their advice. Together with his friend Phil Charig, who had written the music for *Nikki*, he packed the open-topped Packard and set off across the United States for Hollywood. They arrived shortly before Thanksgiving and booked themselves into a suite at the Château Elysée. Billy Grady had arranged for Archie to see an agent at William Morris, who in turn introduced him to Marion Gering, a Broadway stage director now directing films. Gering liked Archie and invited him to a dinner party given by B.P. Schulberg, the head of production at Paramount.

At Schulberg's dinner, Gering told Archie Leach that he was to direct a screen test of his wife the next day. Schulberg interrupted. 'Why don't you make it with her? She'll need someone to act against. You only have to feed the lines. Nothing too difficult.' There was nothing that Archie Leach wanted more. Driving back to his hotel down Sunset Boulevard, he resolved to make sure the camera caught his right profile and did not make his size seventeen and a half collar seem too big. Hollywood was the dream factory, a city where anyone could become anything they wanted. He did not intend to miss the opportunity.

The test at Paramount Publix's studios on Marathon Street, just in front of the Hollywood Cemetery, went exactly as he had planned. Mrs Gering was a little too flustered to make the most of her screen test, but the young man opposite her was very careful to keep his nerve, and his eye on the camera. A week later Archie Leach was offered a five-year contract by Paramount, starting at $450 a week. 'Only one other thing. You'll need to change your name.'

CHAPTER TWO • DARK VENUS

W

When Archie Leach walked on to the Paramount lot in January 1932, Hollywood's streetcar was certainly packed with stars. Greta Garbo, Charlie Chaplin, Douglas Fairbanks, John Gilbert, Mary Pickford, Adolphe Menjou, Gloria Swanson and Gary Cooper all had their seats. He was simply to become one of the standing passengers, one of the studio's contract players, but he knew he could not even be that as Archie Leach. Universal had just proved the importance of a good name with the release of *Frankenstein*, starring another Englishman, William Henry Pratt, whom the studio had rechristened Boris Karloff. Paramount's chief, Adolph Zukor, had told Frank Cooper that he needed a new Christian name, and suggested a town in Indiana — Gary. Archie Leach simply had to have a new name.

'Becoming a movie star is like getting on a streetcar. Call it Aspire. Actors and actresses are packed in like sardines. There's only room for so many, and every once in a while, if you look back, you'll see that someone has fallen off.... Gary Cooper is smart, he never gets up to give anybody his seat.'

Fay Wray's husband John Monk Saunders suggested he call himself Cary Lockwood, after his character in *Nikki*, but Paramount pointed out firmly that there already was a Harold Lockwood in Hollywood. 'We need something short, sharp and easy to remember, like Garbo,' the studio told him. 'A secretary came in with a list of surnames and put it in front of me,' he recalled later, 'Grant jumped out at me, and that was that.' Cary Grant became the name at the top of Archie Leach's first Hollywood contract.

B.P. Schulberg particularly liked the new name, but not simply because it was short and sharp. It was also uncannily close to Gary Cooper, and he planned to use his latest contract player as a new version of his most popular leading man. Schulberg also hoped that Grant would make Cooper just a little nervous. The six-foot-two-inch former cattle rancher, who had made twelve pictures for Schulberg the previous year, was giving Paramount trouble. He had stomped off on safari to Africa and was refusing to come back unless he got the right to choose which pictures he made. Cooper had been gone four weeks when Paramount announced that they had signed Cary Grant. As the fan magazine *Photoplay* noted, 'Cary looks enough like Gary to be his brother. Both are tall,

HOLLYWOOD'S 'NEW GARY COOPER', OPPOSITE JEAN HARLOW IN *SUZY* IN 1936 (*LEFT*), AND ONLY TOO HAPPY TO POSE FOR HIS FIRST FAN MAGAZINE PHOTOGRAPH (*ABOVE RIGHT*).

Variety's 'potential femme rave' in 1932: with Thelma Todd in *This Is the Night* (above) and Carole Lombard in *Sinners in the Sun* (below).

they weigh about the same and they fit the same sort of roles.'

Paramount did not delay launching their new signing on the screen. They cast him as the tall, dark and handsome hero in a film version of a Broadway play, Avery Hopwood's *Naughty Cinderella*, which they had decided to retitle *This Is the Night*. Grant was to play an Olympic javelin thrower whose frequent travels left his young blonde wife, played by Lili Damita, plenty of time for romance with his other co-star, Roland Young. The experience of filming, however, filled Cary Grant with dread. As soon as the movie was finished, he called a friend to say, 'I'm checking out fast. I've never seen anything so stinkeroo in my life, and I was worse.' It was not to be the last

time that he would fear the worst before a film opened, nor was it the last time he was wrong. When *Variety* saw an early preview, it called him 'a potential femme rave'.

A relieved Cary Grant joined the cast of *Sinners in the Sun*, supporting Carole Lombard. This time he was required to wear white tie and tails. He looked suitably glamorous, but even that could not save the picture. One critic summed it up as 'a weak picture with an unimpressive future before it'. But even before it was released Grant was making *Merrily We Go to Hell*, with Fredric March, another story of unrequited love in luxurious surroundings. This time Grant played the leading man in a Broadway play. The critics were equally unimpressed.

FOREVER IN BLACK TIE OR
WHITE TIE AND TAILS: HERE
IN BLACK WITH CHARLES
LAUGHTON AND TALLULAH
BANKHEAD IN *THE DEVIL
AND THE DEEP* IN 1934.

While Cary Grant had been making three films in five months, Adolph Zukor had been patching up his differences with Gary Cooper, and in May 1932 Paramount's biggest star made a suitably regal return to Hollywood, sporting a monkey he had bought in Africa on his shoulder. To celebrate, Schulberg decided to use him in a submarine adventure, *The Devil and the Deep*, opposite Tallulah Bankhead and Charles Laughton in his Hollywood début. Cooper was to play one British lieutenant on board; the other was to be Cary Grant.

As *Photoplay* pointed out, 'They know that they're pitted against each other and when the final gong sounds one of them will be on the floor.' In the event neither was. The film simply marked Cooper's triumphant return. 'The best dramatic talkie we have yet seen,' claimed one reviewer when it opened in August 1932, and *Variety* described its star as 'looking better than he has in a long time'. The critics barely noticed Cary Grant. In the years to come he was to count it as one of the handful of his films that he loathed.

B.P. Schulberg, however, was delighted. To celebrate he decided to make Grant the male lead in a film with his new female star, Marlene Dietrich, to be directed by her lover, Josef von Sternberg. The couple had just finished *Shanghai Express* for him, with another

Englishman, Clive Brook, and both had expressed a preference for 'Britishness' in their leading men. In fact, von Sternberg and Paramount were locked in a bitter argument over the film, which was to be called *Blonde Venus*, because the director wanted one ending and the studio another. When Paramount threatened to fire von Sternberg, he stormed out of Hollywood, only for Dietrich to insist that she would not work with another director. Finally, the dispute settled, filming began in July 1932.

On the first morning von Sternberg suddenly stopped work and took his leading man to one side. As Grant remembered later, 'He grabbed a comb, and parted my hair on the 'wrong' side, where it's remained ever since.' It was the last part of the transformation of Archie Leach into Cary Grant. Now he

looked thinner and a little frailer on the screen, and von Sternberg encouraged his natural diffidence to surface for the first time, making him seem gallant rather than simply flashily handsome. The German director won Grant the best reviews of his career to date. Though not every critic liked the film itself, with its story of a mother who becomes a prostitute to support her only child, they all liked Cary Grant. *The New York Times* in particular suggested he was 'worthy of a much better role'.

The $450 a week Cary Grant was earning was beginning to mount up. He and Phil Charig had moved into a house in West Live Oak Drive, just below the Hollywood sign, and he was investing his money in a men's clothing shop on Wilshire Boulevard called Neale. The investment turned out to be a financial disaster, but the experience taught Grant an important lesson: never to have any debts. Meanwhile, his Hollywood friendships were also beginning to blossom. At Paramount he had been introduced to one of the studio's other contract players, a relaxed, Virginia-born former football star called Randolph Scott, who was a year older than he was. A few weeks later, when Phil Charig decided to go back to New York, Scott came to live with Grant in West Live Oak Drive. The two men's friendship was to last for the rest of their lives.

Randy Scott introduced Cary Grant to another young man who was to remain a friend for forty years. Scott's father had given his son a letter of introduction to a family friend, the young motion-picture producer Howard Hughes, who had arrived in Hollywood in 1925. It had been Hughes who encouraged Scott to settle in California and try his hand at being an actor. And it was Randolph Scott who introduced Hughes to Cary Grant.

On the surface, the three men could hardly have been less alike. The maverick, self-confident Hughes, who had lost a fortune making *Hell's Angels* in 1928,

LEFT: JOSEF VON STERNBERG GAVE GRANT A NEW PARTING FOR HIS HAIR IN BLONDE VENUS WITH MARLENE DIETRICH IN 1932. BELOW: CAROLE LOMBARD, GRANT, DIETRICH AND RICHARD BARTHELMASS PARTYING SOON AFTERWARDS.

but come back to make another with *Scarface* and *The Front Page*; the softly spoken, easy-going Scott; and the self-conscious, wary Cary Grant. But, whatever the outward appearances, the three were remarkably alike. All were distinctly careful with their money, and all were a good deal less comfortable in the company of young women than young men, no matter how it may have appeared to the gossip columns.

To the fan magazines, Cary and Randy were the epitome of Hollywood's new young men, and Paramount did everything they could to polish that image. Pictures of them together at the dinner table, dressed in swimming trunks on the diving board of their pool, at boxing matches on Friday nights, were circulated by the studio, along with Carole Lombard's description of their housekeeping arrangements in the house she christened 'Bachelors' Hall': 'Cary opened the bills, Randy wrote the checks, and if Cary could talk someone out of a stamp he posted them.' In the late summer of 1932 *Silver Screen* took up the refrain: 'Cary is the gay, impetuous one. Randy is serious, cautious. Cary is temperamental in the sense of being very intense. Randy is calm and quiet.'

Naturally enough, Paramount wanted Cary and Randy in a picture together and decided they should star opposite one another in *Hot Saturday*, a film adaptation of Harvey Ferguson's best-selling novel. Grant was to be a rich playboy, just as he had been in *Blonde Venus*, while Scott was to play the leading lady's childhood sweetheart who calls off their marriage at the last

moment because he believes she has been unfaithful. The film could have been just another in the Paramount pipeline, but Cary Grant had learnt from Dietrich and von Sternberg. This time, he watched carefully where the lights were being set up — as he had seen Dietrich do — and he stopped 'acting' ostentatiously, as von Sternberg had told him to. Instead, he allowed the camera to discover him. *Variety* said his performance exercised 'extreme restraint'. It was a technique he was to refine in the years to come.

As soon as *Hot Saturday* was finished, Paramount wanted Grant to go back to work, in a film version of Puccini's *Madame Butterfly*, co-starring B.P. Schulberg's mistress, Sylvia Sidney.

LEFT: GRANT'S CLOSEST FRIEND IN HOLLYWOOD, RANDOLPH SCOTT, IN THE HOUSE THE TWO MEN SHARED. WITH BIRTHDAYS JUST FIVE DAYS APART, THEY STARRED TOGETHER IN HOT SATURDAY WITH NANCY CARROLL IN 1932 (ABOVE).

Grant baulked. He did not think he could sing all that well. Was there no one else they could use? Schulberg insisted, and the filming went ahead in the late autumn. As it turned out, he had been right to resist. 'He sings one song, and it ain't so hot,' *Variety* commented when the film was released on 30 December. But the bad reviews hardly mattered. Four weeks later, at the

'WHY DON'T YOU COME UP
SOMETIME AND SEE ME?'
MAE WEST'S FAMOUS
INVITATION IN *SHE DONE
HIM WRONG* HELPED
GRANT'S SALARY RISE TO
$1,000 A WEEK IN 1933.

end of January 1933, Cary Grant took his first real steps along the Hollywood streetcar, making his eighth film for Paramount, *She Done Him Wrong*, opposite the remarkable Mae West.

West was Broadway's biggest and most voluptuous star, 'buxom, blonde, fat, fair and I don't know how near forty', in the words of the columnist Louella Parsons. In a string of stage shows she had made sex respectable by 'taking it out in the open and laughing at it', and Adolph Zukor had guaranteed her $5,000 a week for ten weeks in 1932 as a result. 'Broadway was in real trouble,' she wrote later. 'Maybe, I decided, I'd take a fling at Hollywood.' *She Done Him Wrong* with Cary Grant was her first film, and her first words on the screen made her a star. She despatched an awestruck hat-check girl who commented, 'Goodness, what beautiful diamonds' with a reply that she had written herself: 'Goodness had nothing to do with it.'

Mae West would claim later that she 'discovered' Cary Grant on the Paramount lot, telling her producer when she spotted him, 'If that man can talk, I want him for my co-star.' But Grant disputed the story, insisting that it had been the director, Lowell Sherman, who chose him, after seeing his performance in *Blonde Venus*. But West gave Grant the opportunity to add another dimension to his appeal. She helped to

make him the man every woman in the cinema audience longed to seduce, allowing him to refine still further his half-surprised, half-knowing reaction, and she used his vaudeville timing to unique effect. For, as well as being Mae West's leading man, Grant became her straight man. 'Haven't you ever met a man who can make you happy?' he asked her. 'Sure, lots of times,' came the reply.

pause, 'Come up. I'll tell your fortune. Aw, you can be had.' Grant's half-raised eyebrow proved forever that he was capable of far more than the straightforward parts he had so far been given by Paramount.

The film took more than $2 million at the American box-office, and helped to pull Paramount out of a dangerous slump. Zukor had been forced to consider a merger with MGM, as well as the sale of Paramount's 1,700 cinemas across the United States, but Mae West and *She Done Him Wrong* meant that he could shelve the plan. Three months later he agreed to pay her $300,000 for her next film, and $100,000 for the screenplay. Somehow he seemed to forget that her co-star was Cary Grant, who was being paid just $750 a week. The memory of Paramount's reaction to the success of *She Done Him Wrong* was to rankle with Grant for years. He felt that the studio had ignored his contribution to the picture, which in turn convinced him that his future lay as a freelance, free to make whatever deals he could with whoever was prepared to pay his price, free to choose the kind of films he wanted to make.

But to Paramount he was still merely a contract player. To prove it, just as *She Done Him Wrong* started to draw crowds across the country and he completed another melodrama with Nancy Carroll called *Woman Accused*, the studio put him into a John Monk Saunders flying story, *The Eagle and the Hawk*, opposite Fredric March. Grant loathed the part, not least because Gary Cooper had turned it down, but he had no choice. In the event, *Variety* proved

She Done Him Wrong passed into Hollywood folklore for its dialogue. 'You know, I...I always did like a man in uniform, and that one fits grand,' West told Grant in his role as the Hawk, a man who is apparently a Salvation Army captain but is actually a government agent. 'Why don't you come up sometime and see me? I'm home every evening.' Then, with just a moment's

he was right, calling the film 'strictly a formula story'. But no sooner had Grant stepped out of his Royal Flying Corps uniform than the studio had him posing as a confidence trickster opposite Benita Hume in *Gambling Ship*. There was nothing he could do to escape.

To add insult to injury, Paramount then insisted that Cary Grant appear in Mae West's second film, *I'm No Angel*, this time as a rich socialite whom she sues for breach of promise when he refuses to marry her. Though he was now earning $1,000 a week, it infuriated him. He believed he deserved better. With fewer of the double entendres that distinguished *She Done Him Wrong*, and

with West herself 'minus the bustle and corsets', in *Variety*'s words, 'something was missing'. Nevertheless, when it was released in October 1933, *I'm No Angel* still earned Paramount $2 million at the American box-office.

Off the set, Cary Grant meticulously protected the image Hollywood had given him. He might argue in private with Paramount about the films he was asked to make, but he knew what was required of a star in the making. He sunbathed whenever he could to keep a tan, avoided being photographed smoking (although he smoked thirty or forty cigarettes a day), did not wear a hat (because Schulberg felt it did not

suit him) and chose whom to be seen with in public with considerable care. One young woman he was seen with increasingly in the spring of 1933 was Virginia Cherrill, a striking blonde from Chicago. Cherrill had become a star just two years before, playing the blind flower girl in Chaplin's silent masterpiece *City Lights*. She was effervescent, uninhibited and completely confident in herself; Louella Parsons

Right: With Noël Coward and Mae West while shooting *I'm No Angel* in 1933.
Below: Back in uniform, opposite Fredric March in *The Eagle and the Hawk*.

THE ACTRESS VIRGINIA
CHERRILL BECAME THE FIRST
MRS CARY GRANT IN
FEBRUARY 1934 IN
LONDON, SHORTLY AFTER
THIS HOLIDAY TOGETHER IN
PALM SPRINGS.

had named her 'Hollywood's greatest beauty'. Grant confessed later, 'I fell in love with her the moment I saw her.'

In the late summer of 1933 Cary Grant and Virginia Cherrill became an item in the Hollywood gossip columns, just as he started work on Paramount's Christmas production. Zukor had decided that the studio needed to make a major family film in the wake of its success with Mae West, and had settled on a new version of *Alice in Wonderland*. Gary Cooper was to be the White Knight, W.C. Fields Humpty Dumpty, Jack Oakie Tweedledum and Zukor wanted Bing Crosby to play the Mock Turtle and sing Lewis Carroll's song about beautiful soup. But Crosby backed out and Zukor cast an unenthusiastic Cary Grant in his place. When the film opened in New York just before Christmas, *The New York Times* called his 'lachrymose Mock Turtle...highly amusing'.

As soon as *Alice in Wonderland* had finished shooting, however, Cary Grant and Virginia Cherrill left Hollywood for England. The crowd of reporters who saw them off thought they were going to get married, but there was another, more significant reason for Grant's first journey across the Atlantic for fourteen years. He was going to see his mother. Elias Leach, who now lived with another woman, Mabel Johnson, with whom he had a son Eric, had finally written to his

SOMEWHAT TO HER SURPRISE,
WHEN THE NEW MRS CARY
GRANT MOVED INTO HER
HUSBAND'S HOUSE IN
HOLLYWOOD, RANDOLPH
SCOTT SEEMED IN NO HURRY
TO MOVE OUT.

son to explain exactly what had happened to Elsie. She was still in the Bristol mental institution to which Leach had sent her almost twenty years before; he suggested that his son might visit her. Cary Grant did not want to make the journey alone.

Cary Grant never talked about what happened when he met his mother again after two decades. It was one of the secrets he kept throughout his life,

presumably a memory so painful that he could never bring himself to discuss it. But their relationship seemed to take up almost exactly where it had left off. Archie Leach, the boy who had become Cary Grant, still longed for his mother's approval and was still frightened of her temper. Elsie Leach still seemed determined to give her son the impression that she alone knew best. On 9 February 1934, the day after his mother's fifty-seventh birthday, Cary Grant married Virginia Cherrill at Caxton Hall registry office in London. It was her second marriage, but his first. 'We're both due back in California for work on pictures,' he told the reporters waiting

outside, 'so our honeymoon will be short.' It was. They were back in Hollywood within ten days, and while her new husband started work again for Paramount the first Mrs Grant moved her belongings into his house on West Live Oak Drive. To her surprise, Randolph Scott did not seem to intend to move out.

Grant's new film, *Thirty Day Princess*, in which he was again to star opposite Sylvia Sidney, was no better than many of the others he had been offered. A feeble story of a princess on a goodwill mission to the United States who gets the mumps and has to be replaced by an actress who looks exactly

ALWAYS A PAINSTAKING
PROFESSIONAL ON THE SET:
HERE EXAMINING TESTS FOR
B.P.SCHULBERG'S ROMANTIC
COMEDY *KISS AND MAKE UP*
IN 1934.

Variety described Grant's performance as 'colorless' and 'meaningless'. It was to become another of the handful of films that Grant wished he had never made.

Back at Paramount, Schulberg put him straight into a light romantic comedy, *Kiss and Make Up*, as a beautician who does not realize his plainish secretary, played by Helen Mack, is in love with him until she threatens to elope with someone else. *The New York Times* dismissed it as 'a first-class lingerie bazaar and a third-class entertainment'. Undeterred, the studio made Grant the lead in another feeble story, this time as a philandering Parisian in *Ladies Should Listen*, opposite Frances Drake. That too was a flop, although one critic complimented him on his 'delightful flair for comedy'.

In the four months since his return from England, Cary Grant had made four films and four flops. In despair, he begged to be loaned out to MGM, who were planning a film based on a new book about the mutiny on the *Bounty* in 1789. Irving Thalberg had specifically asked him whether he would consider playing one of the main supporting roles, alongside Clark Gable as Fletcher Christian and Charles Laughton as Captain Bligh, and he desperately wanted to do it. It would give him an opportunity to prove he could do more than wear a white tie and tails. But Adolph Zukor was adamant. He would do what Paramount wanted, when they wanted and with whom they wanted: nothing else. A disappointed Thalberg gave the role to Franchot Tone.

At home in West Live Oak Drive, Cary Grant was heartbroken. But

like her (Sidney played both parts), it called for Grant to be a millionaire newspaper publisher. Once again, he was required to do little more than spend most of his time wearing white tie and tails. When the film was released in May, *Esquire* called it 'a complete dud'. And an infuriated Cary Grant demanded that he be allowed to choose his own roles. Paramount retaliated by lending him to United Artists.

Grant might have been better advised to keep quiet, because the film he made for United Artists, *Born to Be Bad*, with Loretta Young, also demanded that he spend most of his time in white tie and tails, this time as the president of a large company who is sued for knocking down a boy in a road accident. Brutally edited at the last minute, it ended up being what *The New York Times* called 'a hopelessly unintelligent hodgepodge'. To make matters worse,

Paramount's decision was not the only reason. His marriage to Virginia Cherrill, barely seven months old, was turning out to be a disaster. In particular, he had become insanely jealous if she paid any attention to another man. His fear of being deserted by a woman, in the wake of his mother's reappearance in his life, had taken its toll. If they went to one of William Randolph Hearst's parties, for example, he would insist that his wife spoke to no one except him. When he wasn't working he preferred them to spend their time at home, so that he could go through his press cuttings. Even that could drive him into a rage, however, when he came across a bad review or saw Gary Cooper being praised. In the middle of September 1934, Virginia went back to live with her mother,

claiming that her husband was given to 'murderous rages'.

Grant tried to dismiss his wife's departure as nothing more than a 'quarrel, such as any married pair in Hollywood might have'. But by the beginning of October he was drinking heavily, and in the early hours of the 5th he was discovered unconscious with a bottle of pills on the bedside table. An ambulance was called and Grant was taken to hospital, but no traces of poison were found in his stomach. When he finally recovered consciousness he tried to pass the events off as 'a prank'. But some time later he admitted, 'I had been drinking most of the day before, and all that day.... You know what whisky does when you drink it all by yourself. It makes you very sad. I began calling people. I know I called Virginia.... The

next thing I knew they were carting me off to the hospital.'

Paramount despatched a chastened Grant to work on *Enter Madam*, alongside the opera star Elissa Landi. It was the story of an opera singer's stormy marriage, complete with arias. This time Grant was in both black tie and white tie, tuxedo and tails. He was certain the film would be another flop, and he was right. Now the studio put him into *Wings in the Dark*, opposite Myrna Loy, straight from her success as Nora Charles in *The Thin Man*. This time he played a pilot attempting to perfect

THE STUDIO LIKED ITS LEADING MEN TO BE SEEN IN THE COMPANY OF BEAUTIFUL WOMEN. HERE GRANT IS NEXT TO LILI DAMITA, WITH RUBY KEELER AND TOBY WING BEYOND.

December 1934 Virginia Cherrill told a Los Angeles court that Grant 'drank excessively, choked and beat her, and threatened to kill her'. She went on to ask for substantial maintenance payments from the $1,000 a week her husband was receiving from Paramount. The studio were horrified. Their leading men could not afford publicity like that. Grant settled his wife's financial demands out of court, and in January 1935 slipped out of Hollywood for another trip to England. He was still away when Virginia returned to court for the final divorce hearing in March, describing him as 'sullen, morose and quarrelsome in front of guests'. Their marriage had lasted just thirteen months.

When he got back to California, Paramount put him in uniform, as a British officer in *The Last Outpost*, with Claude Rains. Graham Greene was later to describe the film in the *Spectator* as 'a curious mixture. Half of it is remarkably good and half of it quite abysmally bad', but that did nothing to improve Cary Grant's relations with Paramount. He was convinced they would never give him anything of any real value. In the end, it was not Zukor or Schulberg but his friend Howard Hughes who offered him a part that allowed him to demonstrate just how good a performer he could be.

instrument flying who is blinded in an accident and befriended by the stunt-flying Loy. When the film opened in February 1935, *Variety* said his performance 'topped all his past work'.

But the good reviews for his acting were overshadowed by his wife's reviews of his performance as a husband. In

Since his own divorce in 1929, Hughes had been involved with a series of beautiful young actresses, but in the past year had become steadily more and more attracted to the angular, unconventional and independently minded Katharine Hepburn, who had won an Oscar in 1933 for her performance in *Morning Glory*. Both suspicious of strangers and reluctant to waste time on Hollywood's extravagant parties, Hughes and Hepburn shared a passion for aeroplanes. Naturally, Hughes had talked to Hepburn about his friend Cary Grant, and she in turn had mentioned his name to the director of her next project, George Cukor, who was working at RKO. Hepburn wanted to make a film version of Compton Mackenzie's novel, *The Early Life and Adventures of Sylvia Scarlett*, which had been inspired partly by the Crippen murder case. Focusing on the escape from France to England of an embezzler who teams up with a Cockney conman called Jimmy Monkley, the story required Hepburn, as the embezzler's daughter, to spend most of her time wearing a young man's clothes to help them avoid detection. She suggested that Cary Grant should play Monkley. Cukor liked him and recommended him to Pandro Berman, who was to produce the picture for RKO. 'He had no chance at Paramount,' Berman said afterwards. 'He was a failure there. I gave him the part because I'd seen him do things which were excellent, and Hepburn wanted him too.'

An immensely grateful Cary Grant said afterwards, 'For once they didn't see me as a pleasant young man with black hair, white teeth and a heart of gold.... It permitted me to play a character I knew.' Filming began in the summer of 1935, after Edmund Gwenn had been hired to play the embezzler. Grant relished the role of the artful Monkley. As Hepburn herself suggested afterwards, 'George Cukor brought the Archie Leach

ONE OF HOLLYWOOD'S ARISTOCRATS, COUNTESS DOROTHY DI FRASSO, DANCES WITH GRANT AT HER 'RED AND WHITE BALL' IN 1936. INVITED TO WEAR RED AND WHITE, THE GUESTS LATER CHANGED INTO CRÊPE PAPER COSTUMES.

'CHARM MERCHANT' CARY
GRANT TURNS ACTOR AS A
COCKNEY CONMAN FOR
GEORGE CUKOR AND RKO
IN *SYLVIA SCARLETT* IN
1936, THE FIRST OF HIS
FOUR FILMS WITH KATHARINE
HEPBURN.

out in Cary Grant.' Cukor agreed: 'It
was the first time he began to feel that
an audience could like him. He had an
awfully good part, and he suddenly felt
the ground firm under his feet.' When
Sylvia Scarlett opened at the Radio City
Music Hall in New York in January
1936, the critics noticed the change at
once. 'Cary Grant...virtually steals the
picture,' claimed *Variety*, and *Time* was
of the same mind: his 'superb depiction
of the Cockney' almost 'steals the show'.
The New York Times noted loftily, 'Cary
Grant, whose previous work has too
often been that of a charm merchant,
turns actor in the role of the unpleasant
Cockney and is surprisingly good at it.'

But Cary Grant was not in America
to bask in his first important critical success. By the time *Sylvia Scarlett* opened
he was already shooting again, though
not for Paramount. The studio had
agreed that he could go to England to
make a sound version of *The Amazing
Quest of Ernest Bliss*, the story of a man
who inherits £2 million, but decides to
work for a year to prove he can support
himself. His co-star was Mary Brien, a
former beauty queen who had become a
star in 1924 as Wendy in the first film
version of *Peter Pan*. One reason Grant
had accepted the role was that it would
allow him to see his father, who had
been taken ill. In fact, it was the last

time Grant would see him alive. Elias
Leach died on 2 December 1935 at the
age of sixty-two, from what the death
certificate called 'acute septicaemia', but
what his son later called 'a slow break-
ing heart, brought about by an inability
to alter the circumstances of his life'.
Cary Grant was to keep his father's
pocket watch for the rest of his own life.

After the funeral, he brought his
mother to London with him, while he
went back to work. In the evenings he
would try to get to know the tiny,
upright woman who turned her head
away when he bent down to kiss her, but
it was an almost impossible task. Elsie
Leach refused to leave the private world
that had become her own. She and her
son were strangers. When the filming
was finished, Grant settled her into a
small house in Bristol near her surviving
brothers, and set off for California
again. He was to support her for the rest
of her life, but he would never truly
come to know her.

Meanwhile, in Los Angeles,
Randolph Scott had decided to marry
the heiress Mariana du Pont, who was
more than twenty years older than he
was. But he was determined that his life
in California was not going to be
affected. She was to remain in her
native Virginia, while he was not
intending to leave West Live Oak Drive
and Cary Grant. As Louella Parsons
remarked some years later, after the
couple had divorced, 'Scott's marriage
to the du Pont heiress was always a
mystery.' It certainly did not affect his
friendship with Cary Grant — quite
the opposite. Scott and he now felt
affluent enough to lease the beach house

BACK IN ENGLAND IN 1935
TO MAKE *THE AMAZING QUEST
OF ERNEST BLISS*. HIS FATHER
DIED DURING THE PRODUCTION.

that the producer Joe Schenck had built for his wife, the silent star Norma Talmadge, at 1018 Ocean Front on the Pacific at Santa Monica.

The beach house was the one bright spot on the horizon. Early in 1936 Grant had gloomily returned to working for Paramount. The studio had cast him, opposite Joan Bennett and Walter Pidgeon, as a private detective in *Big Brown Eyes*, which was to be directed by Raoul Walsh. As the *Hollywood Spectator* remarked when it was released, he 'seemed slightly ill at ease as the two-fisted detective'. The highlight was the tiny cameo in which Walsh allowed Grant to impersonate a girl on the make. Only then did his talent show through.

Paramount loaned him out again, this time to MGM, to make *Suzy*, the story of a French flyer in love with Jean Harlow, alongside Franchot Tone, the man who had just been nominated for an Oscar in the role Grant had been offered in *Mutiny on the Bounty*. He did his best with the MGM melodrama, but his heart was not in it, although when the film was released Grant's performance convinced the *Hollywood Spectator* that he was something more than just a leading man: 'Since his outstanding performance in *Sylvia Scarlett*, his talents for varied characterizations have been recognized, and in each new venture he makes good.'

That did nothing to repair his strained relations with Paramount. Back at their lot, he was teamed with Joan Bennett again in a newspaper comedy called *Wedding Present*, based on a Paul Gallico story. Grant played a

practical-joking reporter who gets promoted to city editor, only to realize that he loves the girl he has been teasing relentlessly for the first two reels. He kidnaps Bennett on her wedding day and drives off with her in a wagon with 'Insane Asylum' on the side. As *Variety* put it: 'They try hard, but the combination of story, direction and whatnot is pretty much against them.'

But as 1936 came to an end, so too did the five-year contract Cary Grant had signed with Paramount. He had made twenty-one films for them in five years, but was only truly proud of *Sylvia Scarlett* — for RKO. So although Adolph Zukor was offering him $2,500 a week to sign a new contract, Grant refused. 'If I had stayed at Paramount I would have continued to take the pictures that Gary Cooper, William Powell or Clive Brook turned down,' he explained later.

With the help of his agent, Frank Vincent, Grant went to look for a contract that would allow him to make the films he wanted to make. It was a bold move for someone who was not quite a star, but to his relief Harry Cohn at Columbia offered him a two-year, four-picture contract which guaranteed him $50,000 each for his first two films and $75,000 each for the next two, as well as allowing him to work elsewhere. These were substantial sums for a man who had yet to prove he was a real box-office attraction. *Sylvia Scarlett* had been a disaster at the box-office, in spite of Grant's excellent reviews. *The Amazing Life of Ernest Bliss*, which was just opening in the United States retitled *Riches and Romance*, and which had *Variety* applauding his 'deft characterization', certainly did not put Grant on a par with Cagney, Gable or Cooper.

Remarkably, Grant then managed to manoeuvre himself a second contract, this time at RKO. It allowed him to make one film for Columbia, then one for RKO and then one of his own choice, possibly at another studio altogether. It was almost unheard of in Hollywood in 1937, but it meant that he had taken control of his own career in a way that the contract players were not usually able to do. As the two deals were being negotiated, and as evidence of good will, Grant agreed to make a film for both studios.

Columbia's promised well. It was written by Robert Riskin, the author of Frank Capra's award-winning comedies *It Happened One Night* and *Mr Deeds Goes to Town*, and Grant hoped that it might do for him what Riskin's earlier films had done for Gable and Cooper. But he was to be disappointed. Though it was designed to establish him as a comedian, his co-star was the opera singer Grace Moore and, even more significantly, it was directed by Riskin himself, not Capra. *When You're in Love*, as the film was finally called, turned out to be no more than average. The charming Miss Moore sang prettily enough, but there was no magic between her and Grant on the screen. When it opened at the end of February 1937, the critics damned it with faint praise.

By that time, however, Grant had gone to RKO to star in a film biography of the nineteenth-century American entrepreneur Jim Fisk, who had made and lost a series of fortunes by gambling with stocks and bonds on Wall Street. Called *The Toast of New York*, it was to co-star Edward Arnold, Jack Oakie and Frances Farmer. The studio had struggled with the script for months, using two different books and half a dozen writers, but even that could not make the project work. Cary Grant hid his

disappointment by retiring behind his public persona, which did not appeal to his highly strung co-star. Frances Farmer accused him afterwards of being 'an aloof, remote person, intent on being Cary Grant playing Cary Grant'.

Deflated, Grant returned to his Santa Monica beach house and the

TALENTED BUT UNPREDICTABLE: FRANCES FARMER DID NOT CARE FOR HER CO-STAR IN *THE TOAST OF NEW YORK* IN 1937.

companionship of a new young actress. He had briefly fallen in love with one of RKO's biggest stars, Ginger Rogers, for whom Howard Hughes had also fallen, but she had deserted them both, and he had taken up instead with Phyllis Brooks, a feisty blonde who was not in awe of anybody. They were to remain together for the next two years, spending weekends either at Santa Monica or at William Randolph Hearst's castle 150 miles up the coast at San Simeon.

BELOW: ACTRESS PHYLLIS BROOKS BECAME GRANT'S CONSTANT COMPANION AFTER THE BREAK-UP OF HIS FIRST MARRIAGE.
RIGHT: IN TOPPER IN 1937, WITH HOAGY CARMICHAEL, GEORGE HUMBERT AND CO-STAR CONSTANCE BENNETT, HE PLAYED A MISCHIEVOUS GHOST.

In fact it was in Santa Monica that Grant was also to get his next role. His next-door neighbour at the beach was the comedy producer Hal Roach, who had purchased the rights to a new ghost story, *Topper*, with the idea of making it into a film for MGM. He wanted Grant as his star, to play the ghost. Weekend after weekend Roach badgered Grant until he finally agreed. He would do it before his first major production under his new contract with Columbia, which was due to start in May.

Roach had originally approached W.C. Fields to play Topper, the hen-pecked banker who is haunted by his two rich former clients, Marion and George Kerby. But Fields had turned the part down, and Roach had cast Roland Young in his place. Grant suggested Jean Harlow for the part of his wife Marion, but Roach preferred Constance Bennett, who was much less to Grant's taste. Nevertheless, she brought a chemistry to her role as his spectral wife that Cary Grant had not found with Joan Bennett, Grace Moore or Harlow. But he did not care for the film or his performance. It came as no surprise to him when *The New York Times* called it 'rather a heavy consignment of whimsy'.

Though he had now made twenty-nine films in Hollywood, Cary Grant had still not managed to grab his own seat on the streetcar. He was still standing — nearer the front certainly, but not yet established as a star. He was about to meet the man who was going to do as much as anyone else to help him sit down: the amiable, shrewd and unrepentantly eccentric Leo McCarey.

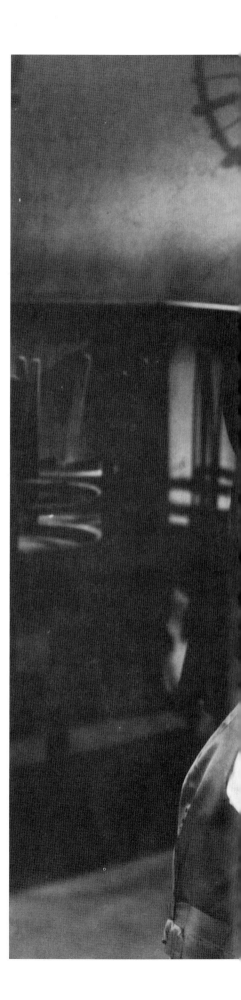

CHAPTER THREE • SCREWBALL

T

Towards the end of his life, Cary Grant liked to tell the story of the old actor on his death bed who was asked how he felt. 'Dying's easy, comedy's hard,' the old man replied. Every time he told the story Grant laughed. He knew exactly how the actor felt. 'People think it's easy to get a laugh,' he would say. 'It's not.' Grant knew only too well that comedy was an enormously serious business, and film comedy was even more serious. He had learnt that from a master of the art: the fey but brilliant Leo McCarey.

'Comedy holds the greatest risk for an actor, and laughter is the reward.'

Born and bred in Los Angeles, the son of a boxing promoter, McCarey had started in the movies immediately after leaving law school and quickly prospered, particularly in comedy. He had brought the best out of the silent comedian Harry Langdon; had gone on to team Stan Laurel with Oliver Hardy in 1924; and directed one of the Marx Brothers greatest hits, *Duck Soup*. Like an old vaudevillian, McCarey relied on inspiration. He would re-write any script as he went along, improvising ideas and jokes as the thoughts struck him.

Like Grant, McCarey had suffered at the hands of Zukor and Paramount,

and he too had left the studio at the end of 1936. By chance, McCarey and Grant joined Columbia at the same time and the studio decided to put them together in a remake of Arthur Richman's 1922 stage comedy *The Awful Truth*, which had been filmed twice before. Typically, McCarey had torn up the script he was given and had started writing another one in his car on the way to the studio in the morning. Alongside Grant, Columbia gave him Irene Dunne, who had just won the studio an Oscar nomination for *Theodora Goes Wild*.

McCarey's habit of arriving on the set each morning with new pages of script did not commend itself to Cary Grant. Shooting had been under way for only a day when he asked if he could swop parts with Ralph Bellamy, and within a week he was offering to do another picture altogether — for nothing — if Harry Cohn would just let him out of *The Awful Truth*. Grant was so uncomfortable with McCarey's methods that he even offered Cohn $5,000 to let him leave the picture. When McCarey heard about it he told Cohn he would give him another $5,000 himself if he would remove Cary Grant from the picture. The studio head simply laughed.

By the second week of shooting, in May 1937, Leo McCarey could barely stand the sight of Cary Grant. Even

LEFT: Never was his eyebrow raised to greater effect than in *The Awful Truth* in 1937, alongside Ralph Bellamy and Irene Dunne. It was a technique he was to use again and again, especially in *Bringing Up Baby* with Hepburn a year later (above right).

DIRECTOR LEO MCCAREY
BROUGHT OUT THE MISCHIE-
VOUS QUALITY BEHIND
GRANT'S FLASHING SMILE,
REVEALING A HUMOUR THAT
OTHER HANDSOME YOUNG
MEN, LIKE HIS STAND-IN ON
THE AWFUL TRUTH, COULD
NEVER QUITE MATCH (*BELOW*).
NOT EVEN A FLANNEL
NIGHTSHIRT COULD
DISGUISE IT (*RIGHT*).

thirty years later he would still remember him as 'impossible', not to mention 'nervous, uncertain and insecure', and Irene Dunne agreed that her co-star could be 'very apprehensive about nearly everything in those days ...so apprehensive in fact he would get almost physically sick'. But gradually it began to dawn on Grant that McCarey was a genius at comedy and, even more importantly, that the director was presenting him with a character that

fitted him more perfectly than anything that he had ever played before.

With McCarey's help, Cary Grant began to reveal to the cinema audience the ambivalence that was to make him one of the cinema's great comedians. As the filming progressed McCarey drew out the mischievous, almost malicious quality that lay beneath the surface of Grant's charm. In his screen relationship with Irene Dunne, Grant even started to reveal the strain of misogynism that was, in fact, part of his own personality. If women were attracted to him, they were never entirely to be trusted, and never to be taken too seriously. Everything a woman said was to be greeted with a raised eyebrow.

His only instructions were to Irene Dunne. On one occasion, he simply told her to open the door of her apartment, discover Grant and say, 'Well, if it isn't my ex.' It was Grant himself who came up with what became the most famous line in the film: 'The judge says this is my day to see the dog.'

McCarey also encouraged Grant to use the physical skill he had learned in vaudeville to make some of the scenes comic without words. At the end of the film, when Grant and Dunne retire to a log cabin to consider their future, McCarey made sure that his male star was discovered on his hands and knees behind his ex-wife's bedroom door wearing only a striped flannel nightshirt. Grant had played the whole scene without a single line of dialogue. When *The Awful Truth* was released in October 1937 it was an instant success. *The New York Times* complimented its 'unapologetic return to the fundamentals of comedy' as 'original and daring', and the *New Republic* called it 'the funniest picture of the season'. The magazine's critic, Otis Ferguson, pointed out that the comedy McCarey had created was 'founded in the commonplace of actual life' and should not be confused with the 'humorous intentions of those who rack their brains for gags, falls, punch lines and the cake-dough blackout'. The film was to win McCarey an Academy Award as Best Director and give Cary Grant an essential part of his personality. The writer and director Garson Kanin believes that in the years to come Cary Grant polished that personality, playing it over and over again — 'each time more skilfully and successfully'.

In *The Awful Truth*, the story of Lucy and Jerry Warriner, a couple on the brink of divorce, McCarey made the story of every man and woman who could live neither together nor apart. Each suspicious of the other's unfaithfulness, they start divorce proceedings — only to fail to agree on who should have custody of their dog.

When their divorce is eventually finalized, they realize that they were happier together than they are apart. The film ends with their reconciliation.

McCarey not only brought an edge to Grant's screen persona, he also gave him the confidence to improvise his own lines. In some scenes McCarey utterly refused to tell Grant what his lines were.

IRENE
DUNNE
CARY
GRANT

The Awful Truth
A COLUMBIA PICTURE

'THE FUNNIEST PICTURE OF
THE SEASON' WON ITS
DIRECTOR AN OSCAR, AND
GAVE ITS LEADING MAN A
PERSONALITY THAT HE WAS
TO POLISH WITH METICULOUS
CARE IN THE YEARS TO
COME.

The success of *The Awful Truth* brought Cary Grant confidence in himself on the screen — a frail confidence, certainly, but one which from then on he would do everything he could to protect. As the film was released, he started work on his first project for RKO under his new deal. The studio's production head, Sam Briskin, wanted him to work with Katharine Hepburn again, and had entrusted a new project to the patrician Howard Hawks, who had recently joined the studio as a producer and director. It was a magazine story written by Hagar Wilde, about a shy palaeontologist and a spoilt New England heiress; it was called *Bringing Up Baby*.

Hepburn's career had not prospered since *Sylvia Scarlett*. She had made a string of flops for RKO, and had taken refuge in a touring stage version of *Jane Eyre*. But she had lost none of her appeal for Howard Hughes. He had followed her stage tour in his private plane, and now wanted the studio to use her again. She was to play the heiress Susan Vance, but it had not been clear at first who should appear opposite her. When the reviews of *The Awful Truth* appeared there was no doubt. RKO would use their new contract player, Cary Grant.

But when Hawks, who had made *Dawn Patrol* and *Scarface* for Howard Hughes, first encountered his leading man and explained the part to him, Grant was far from enthusiastic. 'I wouldn't know how to tackle it,' he told Hawks. 'I'm not an intellectual type.' The director was not to be put off. 'You've seen Harold Lloyd, haven't

you?' he said firmly. 'You're the innocent abroad.'

Unlike Grant, Hepburn was fascinated with her part from the beginning. She was determined to overcome her poor reputation at the box-office, and dragged her reluctant leading man into the film, urging him to help her think up extra pieces of comedy. As a result, it was Grant who invented one of the film's funniest scenes, in which he stands on the back of Hepburn's dress, ripping out a panel, leaving her to walk around naked at the rear until he steps manfully behind her to conceal her embarrassment.

Years later Hepburn called her co-star a generous actor and a good comedian, 'though of course he was also very serious'. Hawks too came to appreciate Grant's subtle gift for comedy. Indeed, he unwittingly also gave Grant another element of his screen persona. During shooting the director suggested that he should 'whinny like a horse' when he got angry, a suggestion which Grant not only took up at once but which he used to great effect in the years to come. At the end of the filming, in December 1937, Hawks called Grant a 'great comedian and a great dramatic actor', a man who could do anything.

One of the things Hawks required Grant to do was to demonstrate his sexual ambivalence. But rather than dress his leading man in a long flannel nightgown, as McCarey had done, Hawks put Grant into women's clothes.

Right: Now regarded as one of Hollywood's great screwball comedies, *Bringing Up Baby* opened to lukewarm reviews in 1938, and lost RKO a fortune.
Below: Grant's performance as the mystified palaeontologist revealed his ability to make a fool of himself – without losing his dignity, or his masculinity.

It was the logical extension of McCarey's attempt to alter his stereotype as a leading man, and it was to add yet another ingredient to Grant's screen image. With Hawks's help he became a hero who is also something of a fool: a man who is never quite what he seems. It was also to lead to one of the film's most often quoted lines, when Cary Grant, dressed as a woman, confronts Hepburn's Aunt Elizabeth, played by May Robson. 'I've lost my clothes,' he tells her sadly. 'Well, why are you wearing these clothes?' she replies. In utter exasperation, Cary Grant shouts, 'Because I just went gay all of a sudden.'

Though it was to become one of the cult comedies of the 1930s, *Bringing Up Baby* opened to lukewarm rather than rapturous reviews. *The New York Times*

UNDETERRED BY KATHARINE
HEPBURN'S NEW REPUTATION
AS 'BOX-OFFICE POISON',
GRANT STARRED WITH HER
AGAIN IN THE FILM OF PHILIP
BARRY'S PLAY *HOLIDAY*.
ONCE AGAIN THE CRITICS DID
NOT APPROVE.

remarked icily, 'Miss Hepburn has a role which calls for her to be breathless, senseless and terribly, terribly fatiguing. She succeeds, and we can be callous enough to hint it is not entirely a matter of performance.' *Time* magazine agreed, suggesting that the slapstick the film contained had been devised 'with the idea that the cinema audience will enjoy (as it does) seeing stagy actress Katharine Hepburn get a proper mussing up'. Within six months the independent cinema owners of America were to compile a list of ten performers whom they considered 'box-office poison'.

Katharine Hepburn's was the first name on the list. *Bringing Up Baby* lost RKO more than $350,000.

The same was certainly not true for *The Awful Truth*. It had become one of the biggest box-office successes of 1937, and when the Oscar nominations for the year were announced in February 1938, Irene Dunne, Ralph Bellamy and Leo McCarey were all on the list. The only person who wasn't was Cary Grant. But the success made Columbia all the more anxious to follow *The Awful Truth* up with another Dunne and Grant comedy, and they decided to make a new version

of Philip Barry's 1928 Broadway play *Holiday*. The only snag was that Leo McCarey was reluctant to work with the two stars again so soon. The studio turned instead to George Cukor, who was just finishing *Camille* with Garbo at MGM. When he arrived at Columbia, however, Cukor promptly demanded a new female star. He did not want Irene Dunne to play the sharp-witted socialite Linda Seaton; he wanted Katharine Hepburn.

After a tussle, Cukor got his way, and when she heard the news the gentle Dunne 'cried the entire weekend'. It was not be to Cukor's only blunt decision. He also insisted that Cary Grant revert to stereotype as Johnny Case, a young man who decides he does not want to make any more money, but instead wants to enjoy his life. Cukor dismissed the ambiguity that McCarey and Hawks had brought out of Grant, preferring instead that he act merely as a straight man to Hepburn.

So although Cary Grant's new-found confidence showed on the screen in *Holiday*, the film did nothing to deepen the screen personality that had been forged over the past year. This provoked the critic Otis Ferguson to call it 'mechanical and shrill' when it was released in June 1938, and *The New York Times* doubted whether anyone could put up with Hepburn's 'intensity', even 'so sanguine a temperament as Cary Grant's Johnny Case'. The film failed to become the hit that Columbia had been hoping for.

But that did nothing to dent Cary Grant's box-office appeal. From being a promising young leading man, he had now become a star. He was receiving 1,400 fan letters a week and had earned more than $150,000 in the past year. Encouraged by Randolph Scott, he had been quietly investing his money in shares, and now he increased his holdings substantially. In the years to come he would spend as much time studying the *Wall Street Journal* on the set as he would studying his script. Grant had no wish to be poor again. The profitability

of each of his films, and his percentages, were as important to him as the reviews.

Suddenly Cary Grant was more in demand than he had ever been. Even if *Bringing Up Baby* had not been a great success, RKO still wanted to capitalize on their new star. As soon as he finished *Holiday*, the studio asked him to play the lead in an action adventure inspired by Rudyard Kipling's poem 'Gunga Din' and written for them by Ben Hecht and Charles MacArthur. The studio had originally intended that Howard Hawks should direct, but the experience of his slowness on *Bringing Up Baby* put them off and they decided to replace him with cameraman-turned-director George Stevens, who had a reputation

for being fast, economical and easy to work with.

Grant was to play Ballantine, one of three practical-joking British army sergeants in India at the centre of the story. But before shooting began he agreed with Douglas Fairbanks Jr, who was to be one of two his co-stars (the other was Victor McLaglen, who had won an Oscar for *The Informer* at RKO), that they would switch roles.

MORE IN DEMAND THAN EVER, GRANT WENT ON TO STAR IN *GUNGA DIN* FOR DIRECTOR GEORGE STEVENS AT RKO, ALONGSIDE VICTOR McLAGLEN, DOUGLAS FAIRBANKS JR AND ROBERT COOTE.

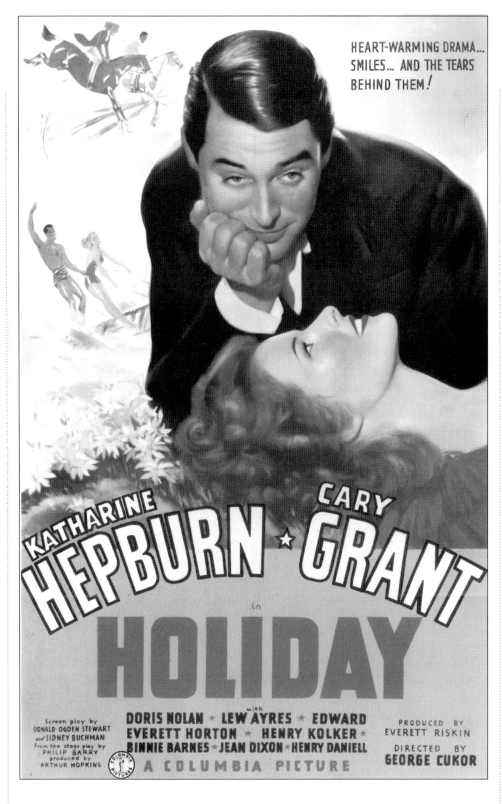

HEART-WARMING DRAMA...
SMILES... AND THE TEARS
BEHIND THEM!

KATHARINE
HEPBURN ★ CARY GRANT
in
HOLIDAY

Screen play by
DONALD OGDEN STEWART
and SIDNEY BUCHMAN
From the stage play by
PHILIP BARRY
produced by
ARTHUR HOPKINS

with
DORIS NOLAN ★ LEW AYRES ★ EDWARD
EVERETT HORTON ★ HENRY KOLKER ★
BINNIE BARNES ★ JEAN DIXON ★ HENRY DANIELL

A COLUMBIA PICTURE

PRODUCED BY
EVERETT RISKIN

DIRECTED BY
GEORGE CUKOR

GRANT CONCEDED TOP
BILLING TO HEPBURN IN
1938; IT WAS THE LAST
TIME HE WOULD DO SO.

persuaded Stevens to allow him to call his character Archibald Cutter.

Shooting began at Lone Pine, California, in June 1938, and RKO assembled no fewer than 1,500 actors, featured players and extras at the largest location camp in Hollywood's history, helping to make the film one of the most expensive the studio had ever made. *Gunga Din* took 104 days to complete, seventy-five of them on location, at a cost of almost $2 million. Nevertheless, it earned the studio more than $3 million, in spite of the fact that its overseas release was hampered by the outbreak of war. This straightforward adventure story, which the *Nation* dismissed as 'spectacular' but also 'a fraud', took more money at the American box-office when it was released in 1939 than *The Wizard of Oz*. It also confirmed Cary Grant's place as one of Hollywood's biggest box-office stars.

As soon as the filming of *Gunga Din* was over, in October 1938, Grant sailed for England to see his mother. War with Germany seemed inevitable, and he wanted her to consider joining him in the United States, not least because he was actively considering becoming an American citizen. Elsie Leach listened quietly as her son explained his plans, but she refused to budge. Only a month earlier Neville Chamberlain had insisted that there would be peace in our time, and she believed him. She had no wish to leave her home. Grant ruefully accepted defeat and sailed back to New York on his way to California and his next picture for Columbia. He was to work again with Howard Hawks.

The new Hawks project, *Plane*

Instead of Ballantine, Grant wanted to play Cutter, an eccentric Cockney. He had no wish to repeat his experience with *Holiday* and be little more than an orthodox leading man. He wanted to add something to the role. He even

IN 1939 IT WAS CARY GRANT'S NAME FIRST ABOVE THE TITLE, FOR BOTH RKO (*ABOVE*) AND COLUMBIA (*BELOW*).

him 'perfectly cast' and praised the film for easily outranking 'most of its plane-crashing, sky-spectacular predecessors'.

It was also the film that many believe gave Cary Grant his most often imitated line of dialogue, 'Judy, Judy, Judy'. The director Peter Bogdanovich suggests that because Grant's girlfriend in the film, played by Columbia's new discovery, Rita Hayworth, was called Judith, he was constantly saying lines like 'Come on, Judy', 'Now, Judy' and 'Hello, Judy', which created the myth that he said, 'Judy, Judy, Judy.' Grant himself could not recall ever saying the line in the film, and wondered instead whether he might have said it in an advertisement he made

Number Four, offered Grant the opportunity to play a dramatic role as the man in charge of a tiny airline running mail across the Andes. Hawks wanted the men in his picture to be tough professionals, playing down the danger in their own lives, while the women were to match their toughness. It was a theme to which Hawks would return time after time in his films, but it also allowed Grant to demonstrate his depth on the screen, underlining once again how far he had come from the flashy young leading man at Paramount. He also did not get all the jokes: the wisecracks were given to his co-star, Jean Arthur.

Adapted by Jules Furthman from a Hawks story, *Only Angels Have Wings*, as the film was eventually retitled, allowed Cary Grant to show that he could hold a scene without attempting to 'act' and that he was not afraid of competition from his co-star. When it was released in May 1939, *Newsweek* called

COLUMBIA'S LATEST
DISCOVERY, RITA HAYWORTH,
AS 'JUDY' IN *ONLY ANGELS
HAVE WINGS*.

for the Lux Radio Theatre, when Judy Garland was to appear. But like 'Play it again, Sam', 'Judy, Judy, Judy' became one of Hollywood's myths, a line that everyone believes they heard on the screen, but never actually did.

After *Only Angels Have Wings* was completed, Cary Grant duly applied for American citizenship before returning to RKO. The studio had planned that he should do another comedy with Leo McCarey, *Once Upon a Honeymoon*, alongside Ginger Rogers. But McCarey had suddenly been taken ill and at the last moment the studio put Grant into a drama about a loveless marriage called *In Name Only*, directed by John Cromwell and based on a screenplay by Richard Sherman. Grant was to play Alec Walker, a wealthy landowner whose wife (Kay Francis) has married him for his money, and who then falls in love with a widow who has taken a house on his estate for the summer (Carole Lombard). The two women compete for Grant's affection, until in the final reel it is Lombard's love that saves him from pneumonia.

The new film made Cary Grant nervous, however. It was neither a comedy nor an action adventure, and he fretted that it might affect his new-found appeal at the box-office. After filming was finished he moped around his house on West Live Oak Drive, convinced that he had made a dreadful mistake, then took off on another trip to England to see his mother. While he was away he decided to have his front teeth capped to enable him to open his mouth and smile on the screen a little more than he had in the past.

When *In Name Only* was released in August 1939, the critics confirmed

some of his fears. *Time* magazine noted, '*In Name Only* will puzzle cinemagoers who thought they knew just what high jinks to expect when screwball Cary Grant falls in love with screwball Carole Lombard', but went on to describe it as a 'mature, meaty picture'. Graham Greene in the *Spectator* added, 'This is a well made depressing little picture of unhappy marriage. It is often sentimental, but the general picture which

RIGHT: HIS ROMANCE WITH PHYLLIS BROOKS TEMPTED THE AMERICAN PRESS TO PREDICT MARRIAGE AFTER THEIR TRIP TO FRANCE IN JULY 1939. BELOW: BACK IN HOLLYWOOD, HE WORKED WITH CAROLE LOMBARD FOR DIRECTOR JOHN CROMWELL ON IN NAME ONLY.

remains is quite an authentic one — a glossy photographic likeness of gloom.'

By then Cary Grant was suffering his own form of gloom. His relationship with Phyllis Brooks, which had been part of his life for two years, was suffering its own difficulties. They had travelled round Europe together in the summer of 1939, ending up at the Roman villa of Hollywood hostess Dorothy di Frasso, a place where many other stars had visited. The trip had been widely reported in the gossip columns. This, in turn, had infuriated Phyllis's distinctly Victorian mother. In Europe, Grant and Brooks had even discussed getting married, and when he got back to California he had a prenuptial agreement drafted. One of its provisions was that Phyllis's mother should never be allowed to set foot in their house. When Phyllis, then twenty-four but still living with her parents, told her mother, there was a furious row and Phyllis sided with her parents.

Grant retreated to Columbia to make his third film in three years with Howard Hawks. The director wanted to remake the Hecht and Macarthur newspaper comedy *The Front Page*, which

ROSALIND RUSSELL WAS
GRANT'S CO-STAR IN
HOWARD HAWKS'S *HIS GIRL
FRIDAY* IN 1940. SHE
TRADED WISECRACKS WITH
HIM LINE FOR LINE, AND
BECAME ONE OF HIS CLOSEST
FRIENDS.

had first been made into a film by
Howard Hughes in 1931. But this time
Hawks wanted Hildy Johnson, the
reporter who decides to leave a Chicago
newspaper and its ruthless city editor
Walter Burns, to be a woman rather
than a man. In Hawks's new twist,
Hildy was to be divorced from Burns
and intent on marrying a naïve insurance
agent, when Burns tried tempts her back
to her old job one last time. Grant was
to play Burns, and Hawks had tried to
persuade Jean Arthur, Irene Dunne and
Claudette Colbert to play Hildy. They
had all refused and he finally persuaded
Rosalind Russell, a Catholic lawyer's
daughter from Connecticut, to consider
the role. Russell liked the idea, but she
also realized that her co-star was going
to get the funniest lines. Without telling
Hawks, she hired an advertising copy-
writer to help her improve her dialogue.

When shooting began in early
September 1939, Grant suddenly found
himself in fierce competition with
Russell. His natural arrogance, on which
Hawks had capitalized in *Only Angels
Have Wings*, once again underscored his
performance, but this time he was not
allowed to get away with it. Although
Hawks had been encouraging him to
ad-lib some of his dialogue, he now
found himself opposite a co-star who
was ad-libbing hers, often to funnier
effect. Grant was so taken aback that at

ABOVE: HOWARD HAWKS
ENCOURAGED HIM TO AD-LIB
IN *HIS GIRL FRIDAY*.
BELOW: GRANT'S FRIENDSHIP
WITH ROSALIND RUSSELL SAW
HIM ACT AS BEST MAN AT
HER WEDDING TO FREDDIE
BRISSON.

around on corrupt errands' at 'break-neck speed', in the words of the critic Pauline Kael.

During the filming Grant and Russell became friends. She went out with him on Saturday evenings as his relationship with Phyllis Brooks stumbled from crisis to crisis. 'It wasn't that we didn't love each other,' Brooks explained later. 'It was just the ghastly situation.' When Brooks's London agent, Freddie Brisson, came to stay with Grant and Randolph Scott over Christmas in 1939, Grant introduced the agent to his co-star. Within two years he was to be the best man at their wedding.

The chemistry between Grant and Russell, and their respect for one another as comedians, communicated itself to the audience. When *His Girl Friday* was released in the first weeks of 1940, *Variety* described him as doing his role 'to a turn', and *The New York Times* added, 'Cary Grant's Walter Burns is splendid, except when he is being consciously cute.' The *Nation*

and Russell rushed into their lines, rarely leaving each other a moment to breathe. As a result the film is one of the fastest-moving comedies ever made in Hollywood, with line overlapping line, gag overlapping gag, as a 'vanished race of brittle, cynical, childish people rush

one point during the filming he looked across to Hawks behind the camera and asked with a pained expression, 'Is she going to do that?' The director liked the remark so much that he left it in the final cut of the film. As a result, *His Girl Friday*, as Hawks rechristened *The Front Page*, included many of Rosalind Russell's own additions to the script, not least her response to Grant's line 'Some day that guy's going to marry that girl and make her happy.' Russell paused just a moment before ad-libbing briskly, 'Sure. Slap happy.'

With Hawks's encouragement, Grant

complimented both stars on their
'entertaining performances', while
another critic called them 'hardened
skunks (but softies underneath)'.

By then Grant was back at work for
RKO. *Once Upon a Honeymoon* was
still on hold, this time because Ginger
Rogers was not free to do it, and in its
place Leo McCarey had started work on
a new project for Grant and Irene
Dunne. Written by Bella and Samuel
Spewack, *My Favorite Wife* was based
on the age-old story of a man who

remarries only to discover that the wife
he believed had died seven years earlier
is, in fact, alive. And not only alive, she
has spent the intervening years living on
a desert island with a handsome
scientist. The ever-mischievous McCarey
cast Randolph Scott as the scientist,
alongside Grant and Dunne as the
long-separated husband and wife.

Just before shooting started,
however, McCarey was badly hurt in a
car accident, and in his place RKO
rapidly appointed Garson Kanin, then a

REUNITED WITH IRENE DUNNE
IN *MY FAVORITE WIFE*,
GRANT WAS SOON BACK IN
A BEDROOM SCENE – THIS
TIME IN HIS WIFE'S DRESSING
GOWN.

twenty-eight-year-old writer and director,
who had just finished making a film with
Ginger Rogers. Dunne was costing them
$150,000 and Grant $112,500 plus
two and a half per cent of the producer's
revenue, and the studio were anxious to
press on as quickly as possible. McCarey

IRENE DUNNE CARY GRANT

MY FAVORITE WIFE

became the film's producer, although not long after shooting started he began to turn up to see what was going on.

As Garson Kanin was to admit many years later, no matter how carefree and easy-going Cary Grant may have appeared on the screen, on the set he was a serious and concentrated professional. But for the performance itself, Kanin realized that Grant relied on his instinct. 'I don't recall him ever intellectually discussing a role or a scene or a picture or a part.' Like Hawks, Kanin sensed that Grant could also be funny wearing women's clothes, and saw to it that in *My Favorite Wife* he was discovered both in his

ex-wife's hat and dress and in his new wife's leopard-skin dressing gown.

The New York Times liked the result. 'A frankly fanciful farce,' its critic Bosley Crowther commented. 'A rondo of refined ribaldries and an altogether delightful picture with Cary Grant and Irene Dunne chasing each other around most charmingly in it.' *Time* magazine agreed, although it commented that, at times, the film 'tends to get bedroomatic and limp, but it pulls itself together in scenes like those in which Cary Grant scampers between his wives' hotel rooms pursued by the distrustful but admiring clerk'. It went on to become one of RKO's most successful films of 1940,

DUNNE WON TOP BILLING IN 1940 – BUT HE WAS NEVER TO SURRENDER THE POSITION TO ANYONE AGAIN, MAN OR WOMAN.

earning more than half a million dollars in profit and extending still further Cary Grant's run of box-office successes.

The only cloud on the horizon was that his relationship with Phyllis Brooks finally came to an end as the filming finished. To cheer himself up, Grant decided to take a trip by steamer through the Panama Canal and up the east coast of the United States to New York, where he was to meet Howard Hughes. By the time he got back to Hollywood, Phyllis had left for New York, where she was to stay for a year. Her mother was sure that she had saved her daughter from the biggest threat in her life.

As soon as he returned to Los Angeles, Grant reported back to Columbia. He had made four pictures for the studio since signing his contract in 1937, but now he wanted new and better terms, and the opportunity to extend his range. Harry Cohn immediately suggested that he might consider making a costume drama. The studio had acquired the rights to the 1939 bestseller *The Tree of Liberty* by Elizabeth Page, a sprawling 985-page story of a Virginia backwoodsman who marries the daughter of an aristocratic family and becomes entangled in the American War of Independence. MGM's *Gone with the Wind* had convinced Cohn that there was an apppetite for costume drama, and he believed this might satisfy it. After some heart-searching Grant agreed, and together he and the studio set out to find a co-star. They chose the twenty-six-year-old Martha Scott, who had made just one previous film, *Our Town*, based on Thornton Wilder's play. Scott was not sure exactly why she had been chosen, although she was to suggest years later that it was because she looked very like the young woman Grant had just met for the second time, and who was destined to be his second wife: the Woolworth heiress Barbara Hutton.

Grant had first been introduced to the tiny blonde Hutton when they were passengers together on the liner *Normandie* as it returned to New York from England in June 1939, and they had been reintroduced by his old friend Dorothy di Frasso. Hutton had decided to settle in California now that she was separated from her second husband, Count Reventlow, and she had moved into a house in Beverly Hills. Di Frasso, whose long affair with Gary Cooper had been replaced by an equally intense relationship with the gangster Bugsy Siegel, thought that Hutton and Grant might make an ideal couple. Unlikely as it may have seemed, they had begun to see each other regularly by the time he began work on his new film for Columbia.

In spite of Harry Cohn's hopes, the uniform and the pony-tail Grant was required to wear for *The Howards of Virginia*, as *The Tree of Liberty* was retitled, did not make him feel in the least at ease. He was uncomfortable in the costumes, and he found it almost impossible to obliterate the screen character he had spent so much energy creating. Though he struggled to submerge the rich, slightly misogynist quality of Walter Burns, he never quite managed to, and thereby made his

COLUMBIA'S HARRY COHN WANTED TO MAKE A COSTUME DRAMA IN 1940 TO RIVAL DAVID O. SELZNICK'S *GONE WITH THE WIND* AT MGM. GRANT WAS TO BE HIS CLARK GABLE.

VASTLY UNCOMFORTABLE
IN HIS PERIOD COSTUME
AND PONY-TAIL, GRANT
STRUGGLED AS THE VIRGINIA
BACKWOODSMAN WHO
ENTERS POLITICS IN *THE
HOWARDS OF VIRGINIA*,
OPPOSITE MARTHA SCOTT.

performance as the surveyor Matt
Howard both less romantic and less
heroic than it should have been.

Although adapted by Sidney
Buchman and directed by Frank Lloyd,
Cary Grant's new costume drama
proved to be neither epic enough nor
dramatic enough for the audience. When
it was released in September 1940,
Newsweek suggested politely that it
came to life 'all too infrequently' and
described Grant as 'obviously miscast'.
In *The New York Times*, meanwhile,

Bosley Crowther pointed to the 'familiar
comic archness' in his performance as
'quite disquieting in his present serious
role...he never quite overcomes a
bumptiousness which is distinctly
annoying'. It was to be almost twenty
years before he would risk appearing in
another costume drama.

Cary Grant learned from his
mistake. He took refuge in a project
that Howard Hughes and Katharine
Hepburn had been trying to set up in
Hollywood for almost a year. Philip
Barry, the author of *Holiday*, had
written a new play, *The Philadelphia
Story*, specifically for Hepburn, which
had been a great success on
Broadway. Now Hughes wanted to
turn it into a film. But Hepburn's
reputation as box-office poison

meant that the studios were distinctly
cool about the prospect.

After a good deal of wrangling,
Hughes, who had bought the rights for
Hepburn, and George Cukor, whom
Hepburn had recruited as the director,
finally managed to persuade Louis B.
Mayer that MGM should take the risk.
The studio boss gave control of the
project to a thirty-one-year-old
producer with ambitions to become a
director, Joseph L. Mankiewicz, and
Cukor agreed that Philip Barry's friend
Donald Ogden Stewart should be called
in to write the screenplay, just as he
had done for *Holiday*. James Stewart,
the drawling, gangling star of *Mr Smith
Goes to Washington* and *Destry Rides
Again*, was cast as the reporter sent to
cover the society wedding of a spoilt

heiress getting married for a second time. Hepburn was to repeat her role as the heiress and Cary Grant was to play her ex-husband, C.K. Dexter Haven.

Filming began in July 1940 and took almost three months. Cukor did not give any of his stars precise instructions; instead he left each of them to work out their own approach to their character. This brought the best out of Cary Grant's new confidence in himself and

GRANT'S THIRD COLLABORA-
TION WITH DIRECTOR
GEORGE CUKOR, ONCE
MORE ALONGSIDE KATHARINE
HEPBURN, RESULTED IN ONE
OF HOLLYWOOD'S BEST-
LOVED SCREWBALL COMEDIES,
THE PHILADELPHIA STORY.

his ability to play comedy. He grabbed every opportunity to improvise, and James Stewart followed his example. Nowhere was that more obvious than in the scene in which Stewart has had too much to drink and comes to wake up Grant. The two men sat opposite each other, and without warning Stewart started to hiccup. Grant's response was instinctive. 'Excuse me,' he said without a flicker of an eyelid, prompting Stewart to say, 'I have the hiccups.' Not a word of the dialogue was in the script.

In *The Philadelphia Story* Cary Grant took elements of Jerry Warriner in *The Awful Truth* and Walter Burns in *His Girl Friday*, and delicately moulded

them into a leading man who was both knowing and yet vulnerable, a man the audience would *will* to end up marrying his ex-wife again in the film's finale. He also allowed his co-stars to deliver showier performances than his: the spoilt Hepburn slowly realizing that perhaps she has made a series of mistakes, the principled Stewart recognizing that being rich is not a handicap to being human. Grant never once stole their limelight. His lines were sharp and funny, but the jokes were not the point; he provided the emotional heart of the film, the reason that it produced such enormous affection in every audience that watched it. When the film opened

at Christmas, the critics were unanimous. The *Hollywood Reporter* described it as 'the type of entertainment which set a box-office on fire. It has youth and beauty, romance and SEX, and oh what sex!' *Variety* added, a little more calmly, 'The picture is highly sophisticated and gets a champagne sparkle, jewel-polish job of direction by George Cukor.' Even Bosley Crowther in *The New York Times* did not quibble, writing that the film had 'just about everything that a blue-chip comedy should have — a witty romantic script... the flavour of high society elegance... and a splendid cast of performers'.

Shortly after *The Philadelphia Story* was released, Joe Manckiewicz wrote to Cary Grant, saying that its success was due to him 'in far greater proportion than anyone has seen fit to shout about'. The young producer called Grant's performance 'sensitive and brilliant' and paid tribute to the fact that it provided the 'basis of practically every emotional value in the piece. I can think of no one who could have done as well or given as much.' Mankiewicz felt that Grant's performance had been 'unjustly slighted' in the hysteria that had surrounded Hepburn's triumphant return to Hollywood. So, though he never said so publicly, did Cary Grant.

The director Stanley Donen, who was later to work with Cary Grant on three pictures, believes that his two greatest screen performances ever were in *His Girl Friday* and *The Philadelphia Story*. 'He's thought of as a man who achieved a certain elegance and savoir faire,' Donen explains now. 'But in truth he was a fantastic actor. It's not just the

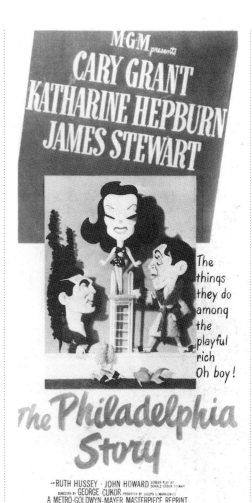

JAMES STEWART WAS IN AWE OF HIS CO-STAR'S ABILITY TO AD-LIB (*LEFT*). WHEN HE PRETENDED TO HAVE THE HICCUPS, GRANT COUNTERED, 'EXCUSE ME.' IT HELPED TO WIN STEWART, AND THE PICTURE, AN ACADEMY AWARD IN 1941.

persona which he had developed over the years; it was his ability to act.' In particular, Donen points to the enormous care Grant took in preparing his performances, making copious notes to himself in the margins of his script. 'He always seemed real. It wasn't a gift from God. It was the magic that came from enormous amounts of hard work.'

ONE OF THE MOST FAMOUS
SCENES FROM HOLLYWOOD'S
GOLDEN AGE: CARY
GRANT'S C.K. DEXTER
HAVEN REMARRIES KATHARINE
HEPBURN'S TRACY LORD IN
THE PHILADELPHIA STORY.

At the Academy Awards ceremony in February 1941, *The Philadelphia Story* won Oscars for both James Stewart and Donald Ogden Stewart, as well as nominations for George Cukor, Katharine Hepburn and Ruth Hussey (for Best Supporting Actress as Stewart's photographer partner). But once again, to his intense disappointment, the one person who was not honoured was Cary Grant. Dispiritedly he donated his fee of $125,000 to the British war effort and set out to find ways of helping the Allied cause. He flew to London to ask what he could do, only to be told to return to Hollywood 'and carry on doing what you do best'. Reluctantly he reported back to Columbia.

The Philadelphia Story was one of the high points of Hollywood's golden age: a comedy which would forever represent elegance and sophistication, and which would never fail to entertain. But, though no one realized it at the time, it was also destined to be one of the last of the sophisticated screwball comedies, the films which had helped to create the persona of Cary Grant on the screen. As Pauline Kael was to suggest many years later, 'After 1940...there were no longer Cary Grant pictures.' That was not entirely true. There just weren't any of those Cary Grant screwball comedies again. A world at war seemed to lack the appetite for that particular concoction of brittle dialogue and high jinks.

CHAPTER FOUR • MR LUCKY?

Cary Grant's relationship with Barbara Hutton deepened steadily during the making of *The Philadelphia Story*, until, as shooting came to end, it became news. In November 1940, *Photoplay* magazine called their romance 'the most hushed up love story in Hollywood', and speculated that they would marry within a year. But neither Grant nor Hutton would confirm or deny the story. They were too nervous about the damage publicity might do.

One reason was that Barbara Hutton, still only twenty-eight, was afraid. The memory of the Lindbergh kidnapping case was all too fresh in Hollywood, and Hutton was frightened in case someone should decide to repeat the crime, making her four-year-old son Lance the victim. She had legally separated from Lance's father, Count Reventlow, two years before, and the boy mattered to her more than anything. She was so desperate to protect him that they lived as virtual prisoners in Buster Keaton's old house in Beverly Hills, surrounded by security guards. 'My money has never bought me happiness,' the woman who had inherited $20 million from her grandfather at the age of five told Grant repeatedly. 'You can't buy love with money.'

Cary Grant sympathized with Hutton and her only son. But when the news of their relationship began to leak out it did not make him popular with some sections of the Hollywood community. Hedda Hopper took particular pleasure in repeating their nickname of 'Cash and Cary'. It was less than fair. Hutton's money was of no interest to Grant. He was too proud to want any part of it. In fact, his independence was part of his attraction for her, as was his affection for Lance; while for Grant, Hutton was a woman who clearly needed his support and protection. Phyllis Brooks had not been like that; neither had Virginia Cherrill. They had been tougher, more capable, career women. Barbara Hutton was a complete contrast; she would let him look after her.

By the time the gossip columns caught up with them, however, Grant was back at Columbia, working again. The studio wanted to team him with Irene Dunne for a third time, in a tearjerker about the break-up of a marriage.

'In the films I made with Hitchcock the humour relieved the suspense. People laugh in the theatre because what's on the screen is not happening to them. I played my role as though it wasn't happening to me. I think that's how I got the audience on my side.'

LEFT: ESTABLISHED AS ONE OF HOLLYWOOD'S BIGGEST STARS, GRANT SIGNS HIS NAME IN CEMENT OUTSIDE THE CHINESE THEATRE. ABOVE RIGHT: MARRIAGE TO HEIRESS BARBARA HUTTON IN 1942 INCREASED HIS FAME.

Called *Penny Serenade*, the film was to be directed by George Stevens, who had worked with Grant on *Gunga Din*. It was based on a screenplay by Morrie Ryskind about a childless couple's efforts to adopt a child, with tragic consequences. The title came from the

In his first drama after a string of comedies, Grant starred again with Irene Dunne in *Penny Serenade* in 1941. It became one of his favourite films.

record that was playing on their gramophone as their marriage came to an end. As ever, Grant dithered over whether or not he should do it, telling Harry Cohn it was 'too serious' for him. Finally he asked to be let out of the picture altogether. Just as he had done with *The Awful Truth*, Cohn flatly refused.

It was a reluctant Cary Grant, therefore, who started *Penny Serenade*, but, once again, the more he worked on the picture the more involved he became. The part of the childless

newspaperman Roger Adams touched a nerve in his own personality, bringing memories of his own childhood and the insecurities of his parents. As filming progressed Grant became steadily more and more emotional, unexpectedly bursting into tears several times during the shooting. Years later one close friend would explain, 'The picture meant a great deal to him — more than probably anyone realized at the time.'

One reason why Cary Grant found *Penny Serenade* so emotional was that he and Barbara Hutton had started to discuss having their own children. 'They're going to be blonde with brown eyes,' he told one friend, and although the filming dragged for seventy-four days, the longer it continued the more fascinated he became by the prospect of fatherhood. Once he and Hutton were married, Lance Reventlow would be his first child, a prelude to a family of his own.

When *Penny Serenade* opened in April 1941, the critics were generous. *Variety* called it 'sound human comedy drama', and the New York *Daily Mirror* added, 'Even better than *The Awful Truth*.' Meanwhile, Otis Ferguson in the *New Republic* described Cary Grant as 'thoroughly good', and went on, 'This is a picture not spectacular for any one thing, and yet the fact of its unassuming humanity, of its direct appeal without other aids, is something in the way of pictures growing up after all; for to make something out of very little, and that so near at hand, is one of the tests of artistry.' The film was also to bring Cary Grant his first Academy Award nomination.

DIRECTOR ALFRED HITCHCOCK
WAS TO REVEAL THE DARKER,
MORE MENACING, SIDE OF
GRANT WHEN THEY WORKED
TOGETHER FOR THE FIRST TIME
ON *SUSPICION* FOR RKO.

Barbara Hutton was not the only new partner who was to change Cary Grant's life at this time. In the first week of February 1941, he embarked on a professional partnership that was to alter the course of his career. He went to work for the manipulative, obtuse and extraordinary genius, Alfred Hitchcock, who had been loaned to RKO by David O. Selznick, the creator of *Gone with the Wind*. Selznick had brought the English-born Hitchcock to Hollywood to direct *Rebecca*, and now Hitchcock was preparing another thriller in the *Rebecca*

mould for RKO. Based on a Frances Iles novel called *Before the Fact*, it concerned a woman who becomes convinced that her husband is planning to kill her. Hitchcock wanted Grant to play the murderer, and his star from *Rebecca*, Joan Fontaine, to play the wife and victim. The film was to be called *Suspicion*. The only difficulty was that RKO flatly refused to have their leading man play a murderer.

'The real ending I had in mind,' Hitchcock explained, 'was that when Cary Grant brings his wife the fatal glass

of milk to kill her, she knows she is going to be killed.' The director wanted the film to end with her writing to her mother to explain that she didn't want to live any more as she loved her husband; but nevertheless naming him as her murderer. She was to leave the sealed letter by her bedside, and before

Joan Fontaine was
Grant's wife, and
potential victim, in
Suspicion in 1941. She
was never sure whether
his charm concealed
murderous intent.

drinking the poisoned milk ask her husband to post it for her. In the last shot of the picture Hitchcock wanted Grant, whistling cheerfully, to go and post the letter. Grant later called it 'the perfect Hitchcock ending'.

What Hitchcock had sensed in Cary Grant was the dark, brooding side to his character, the devil that lurked behind his smooth, efficient charm. McCarey had seen it, and so had Hawks, but they had both used it in comedy. Now, for the first time, Hitchcock wanted to bring that menace to the surface. But he did not intend merely to make Grant into a villain, he also wanted the charm and the humour to remain, thereby making him even more compelling as a murderer. Was he to be trusted or not?

Certainly Grant did not find it difficult to want to kill his new co-star. Within a few days of the start of shooting, Joan Fontaine had become one of the few actresses he would positively dislike. To him, she seemed unprepared and unprofessional. To her, he seemed aloof and distant. Hitchcock, the consummate manipulator of the fragile egos of actors, gleefully let their dislike for one another come through on film, contenting himself with telling his stars to 'move around and see if you can keep from running into each other'. Their mutual antipathy made it only too possible that Cary Grant would end up murdering Joan Fontaine.

ART MIRRORED REALITY ON
SUSPICION: GRANT DISLIKED
HIS CO-STAR (ABOVE); SMALL
WONDER THAT HE LOOKED SO
CONVINCING CARRYING THE
POISONED MILK UPSTAIRS IN
ONE OF THE FINAL SCENES
(RIGHT).

making a profit of $440,000, far more than *Citizen Kane*, which they released in the same year.

Soon after Hitchcock had finished with him, Cary Grant left the United States for a month's trip to Mexico with Barbara Hutton. Her divorce from Reventlow had finally come through, and now that she was free he wanted her to marry him at once. But now, suddenly, she hesitated. She was not sure she wanted to rush into marriage for a third time. Disappointed, Grant accepted her decision and went back to filming again in October 1941. Warner Brothers had offered him a role he coveted — that of the acid-tongued Sheridan Whiteside in the film version of George Kaufman and Moss Hart's play *The Man Who Came to Dinner*. Bette Davis had persuaded the studio to pay $250,000 for the rights as a vehicle for her and John Barrymore, but Barrymore's alcoholism — then in its final stages — had made the studio nervous and Grant had been asked if he might be interested in the part. He was, but Davis was less keen and the part went instead to Monty Woolley, who had played it on Broadway.

Ironically, only a few weeks afterwards, Cary Grant started filming another Broadway hit for Warners. The studio had asked Frank Capra, winner of three Academy Awards for Columbia during the Thirties, to direct a film version of Joseph Kesselring's *Arsenic*

In the end, however, RKO prevented Grant from playing a murderer, insisting that he become simply a man whose wife *suspected* him of murder. Nevertheless, Hitchcock's revelation of the menace that lay behind his dark charm was not lost on the critics. When the film opened at Thanksgiving weekend, 1941, the *New Yorker* wrote, 'Cary Grant finds a new field for himself, the field of crime, the smiling villain, without heart or conscience. Crime lends colour to his amiability.' *Variety* agreed: 'Grant puts compelling conviction into his unsympathetic but arresting role.' The *Hollywood Reporter* carped that RKO's ending hurt the film: 'If this sop of a happy ending was dragged in by the heels, as it appears, its serves only to spoil a great picture.' But the studio's decision did not hurt the film at the box-office. *Suspicion* became the most successful RKO film that year,

and Old Lace, about two old ladies who poison the lonely old men who visit their Brooklyn home. Jack Warner had originally offered the part of the ladies' manic nephew, Mortimer Brewster, to Bob Hope, but Capra had insisted he wanted Grant, and Capra had prevailed. Julius and Philip Epstein had written a script, and Grant had negotiated a deal that allowed $100,000 of his $150,000 fee to be divided between the American Red Cross, the United Service Organization and the British War Relief Association. He was to receive his fee immediately, even though the film itself could not be released until the play's run had been completed in New York.

On the surface, everything seemed to bode well. Shooting started on Warners' giant Number Seven sound stage in the third week of October 1941, with Capra well aware that he had just six weeks of Grant's time. The set was a replica of the Brewster home, complete with a scale model of the Brooklyn Bridge and a graveyard, where, as a joke, one of the tombstones bore the name Archibald Leach. But the fiery Italian-American Capra was not like the laid-back McCarey or the laconic Hawks. Ferocious, determined and interfering, he did not believe in letting his star decide the best way to play a part. Instead he insisted on imposing his own style on Grant, making him act in a faster, more

frenzied way than he had ever done before. Grant found himself overacting, forcing farce into the role, mugging for the camera, playing Brewster more as a slapstick clown than a droll. He hated it.

Grant tried to tell Capra how unhappy he felt with all the double-takes that the director was demanding, but to no avail. The comedy that Capra saw was not the comedy that Grant felt he could deliver. Though the supporting cast, including three of the principals from the Broadway production — Josephine Hull, Jean Adair and John Alexander — alongside Priscilla Lane and Raymond Massey, were excellent, *Arsenic and Old Lace* was to become

one film that he could never bring himself to watch in the later years of his life. 'I was embarrassed doing it,' he explained. 'I overplayed the character... Jimmy Stewart would have been much better in the film.'

A distinctly relieved Cary Grant left the Warners lot on 12 December 1941, less than a week after the Japanese attack on Pearl Harbor. But it was not simply pleasure at being released from Capra's direction, it was also the fact that, with the Americans now drawn into the war, it would not be unchivalrous to announce his intention of becoming an American citizen. It was an announcement that also meant that

WORKING WITH DIRECTOR FRANK CAPRA DID NOT TURN OUT TO BE THE JOY GRANT HAD HOPED IT WOULD (*LEFT*). *ARSENIC AND OLD LACE*, WITH RAYMOND MASSEY AND PETER LORRE (*RIGHT*), NEVER SATISFIED ITS STAR.

he could settle the question of his marriage. Barbara Hutton had been reluctant to marry him while he was still a British citizen, not least because her accountants had advised her that she would risk a substantial portion of her fortune being 'frozen' in London. Once Grant was an American, however, that could not happen.

Before the end of 1941, Grant submitted his naturalization papers and immediately went back to Columbia to work with George Stevens for the third time. The success of *Penny Serenade* had convinced Harry Cohn that he should put the director back together with Grant and Dunne as quickly as possible; the new comedy-drama he had found for them was *The Talk of the Town*. The story concerned a small-town schoolteacher forced to choose between a law professor who dreams of becoming a Supreme Court judge and Leopold Dilg, a rebellious mill worker, whom she hides after he is falsely accused of arson and murder. It was written for the screen by Irwin Shaw and Sidney Buchman. Grant was to play Dilg and Ronald Colman the professor. It was the first time that Grant and Colman, one of Hollywood's longest-standing British-born stars, had ever appeared together. But now it was Grant who was sitting at the front of the Hollywood streetcar: he had top billing. When Irene Dunne dropped out at the last minute, Harry Cohn replaced her with Jean Arthur, Grant's co-star from *Only Angels Have Wings*.

Stevens took the precaution of shooting two different endings for his new film, one in which Arthur decides to marry Colman and the other in which

she chooses Grant, and Columbia asked the preview audiences to decide which one he should use. Hardly surprisingly, the audiences went for Grant. When it was released in August 1942, *The Talk of the Town* became one of the most

GRANT'S SEAT ON THE HOLLYWOOD STREETCAR ALONGSIDE RONALD COLMAN WAS ASSURED. THEY WORKED TOGETHER FOR THE FIRST TIME ON *THE TALK OF THE TOWN* FOR COLUMBIA IN 1942.

successful Columbia films of the year. 'Well turned and witty', in the words of *Newsweek*, 'at its best when it sticks to the middle ground between farce and melodrama'. *Variety* added, 'One of the season's more important entries.'

The Talk of the Town was eventually nominated for an Oscar as Best Picture, although once again Grant's own contribution was overlooked. It was not to be his only Oscar disappointment that year. While *The Talk of the Town* was still shooting, he watched Joan Fontaine win the Oscar as Best Actress for her performance in *Suspicion*, while his performance in *Penny Serenade* was passed over. Even more galling, he was beaten for the Best Actor Oscar by his old rival Gary Cooper, who won for his performance in Howard Hawks's First World War drama, *Sergeant York*. The experience was to give Grant a life-long sensitivity about the Oscars.

At RKO in April 1942, Grant joined Ginger Rogers and Leo McCarey to make the often postponed *Once Upon a Honeymoon*. The studio wanted an anti-Nazi picture, and McCarey had come up with a story which he had written with Sheridan Gibney. Grant was to play a radio correspondent covering the threat of war in Europe, and Rogers a former burlesque star about to marry to an Austrian Baron who is also a secret agent for the Nazi party. Grant was to try to dissuade Rogers from marrying, but on failing he was to travel round Europe after her, trying to get her to see the truth. Grant was enthusiastic. The only stumbling block was the billing.

Ginger Rogers was one of RKO's biggest stars, and she insisted on top billing. But Grant had had top billing over Katharine Hepburn in *The Philadelphia Story*, as well as over Ronald Colman in *The Talk of the Town*, and he was determined not to forgo the position. For a time it even looked as though the film might never happen, until eventually RKO found a compromise. Half the paid advertising would have Rogers at the top, the other half Grant.

ABOVE: AT THE 1942
OSCARS PARTY WITH
ROSALIND RUSSELL. JOAN
FONTAINE PICKED UP AN
AWARD FOR *SUSPICION* WHILE
GRANT LOST TO GARY
COOPER. DISAPPOINTED, HE
WENT TO WORK WITH GINGER
ROGERS IN *ONCE UPON A
HONEYMOON* (RIGHT).

Made between April and July 1942, *Once Upon a Honeymoon* was nothing like as trying an experience for Grant as *The Awful Truth* had been five years earlier. One reason was that McCarey was less interested in improvising comedy, only too aware that what the studio expected was a propagandist film. The result was a well-intentioned piece of professionalism rather than one of McCarey's inspirational comedies.

The New York Times noted the mistake of 'trying to mix romantic comedy with tragedy too stark and real'. *Newsweek* added, 'The result is probably a screen hit, but the attempt to play for both laughs and significance against a terrifying background of Nazi aggression is, on the whole, a little disappointing.'

As soon as *Once Upon a Honeymoon* was finished, Grant intended to join the American Army Air Corps. RKO had applied for his deferment while McCarey was shooting, but Grant was determined to enlist. His naturalization papers finally came through in the middle of June, and on the 26th of that month the man born Archibald Alec Leach in England took the American oath of allegiance before a United States Federal Judge in Los Angeles. On the same afternoon, he formally changed his name to Cary Grant.

Twelve days later, at 12.30 on 8 July 1942, he married Barbara Hutton in the garden of his agent's house at Lake Arrowhead, east of Los Angeles. The bride was twenty-nine and the groom thirty-eight. The ceremony, conducted by a local Lutheran pastor, took just six minutes. Randolph Scott was not there, and neither was Dorothy di Frasso. The only witnesses were Hutton's companion and her maid, together with Grant's secretary and agent. Neither the bride nor the groom thought the marriage was anybody's business but their own. The following morning Cary Grant returned to RKO.

Leo McCarey had given him permission to be one hour late.

Leo McCarey had given him permission to be one hour late.

A month later the War Department notified him that he could enlist on 15 September in Los Angeles. He was then to report to the Officer Candidate School at Miami Beach. But Cary Grant never reached the Officer Candidate School. At the last moment the United States government decided that he was more valuable to them as an actor who could be called upon from time to time to give what they called 'temporary service'. A disappointed Grant issued a brief statement: 'Wherever Uncle Sam orders my utilization to the best purposes, there I will willingly go, as should every other man. I feel that Uncle Sam knows best.'

Grant had hoped he and Barbara could live in his Santa Monica beach house, but she decided that it would be 'too small'. Though she was frightened in the company of strangers, she nevertheless loved to entertain, and wanted nothing more than to give dinner parties nearly every night. She was also accustomed to a staff of almost a dozen, including a companion, a secretary, a valet, a chauffeur, six general servants and a cook. Grant manfully insisted the he would be paying for 'rent and groceries', but he had never considered exactly what that meant and Barbara had never bothered to enlighten him.

To meet the new Mrs Grant's needs, the couple leased a house owned by Douglas Fairbanks Jr in Pacific Palisades. Called Westridge, it stood in twelve acres and had more than enough room for the servants, as well as for Lance, who was now six. Barbara would

NO ONE LOOKED MORE LIKE *MR LUCKY* – THE TITLE OF RKO's NEW COMEDY ABOUT A GAMBLER – THAN GRANT, WHO HAD MARRIED BARBARA HUTTON IN JULY 1942.

play tennis in the morning on the court in their garden, and then ride or swim in the afternoon, but in the evenings she would entertain. For his part, Grant preferred the Sunday evenings when they were alone together. He felt suffocated in a house full of servants and guests.

Slightly uncomfortable, Grant went back to work. RKO were anxious to follow up the success of *Suspicion*, and he had an idea which might make a good picture. Milton Holmes, a tennis professional at the Beverly Hills Club, had written a short story called *Bundles for Freedom* and given it to him to read. It focused on a gambler who decides to launch a gambling ship to dodge the draft, but is then persuaded to change his mind and ferry medical supplies to help the war effort. The theme of redemption appealed to Grant and he persuaded RKO to let Holmes work on the screenplay with Adrian Scott. The studio then attached H.C. (Hank) Potter as director and retitled the picture *Mr Lucky*.

On the set, Cary Grant was as professional as he had always been. 'He knew where the camera was, what he wanted to do and he worked very hard,' his co-star Laraine Day recalled later. 'He had managed to teach himself a lot of tricks, and he used them and taught them to other people. It was a treat to work with him.' But in the evenings everything changed. 'Then he wasn't the

bright cheerful person he had been on the set all day,' Day remembered. 'He was subdued, a completely different person. It was astonishing.' It did not go unnoticed. As early as January 1943, *Photoplay* suggested, 'He gets sudden periods of depression', and Hedda Hopper provided one of the reasons: 'Cary was upstairs cramming twelve solid pages of script into his head. Up at six for a studio call, home late dead tired and was not amused by the upper-crust goings-on around the place.'

In deference to his wife, Grant took a break from films as soon as *Mr Lucky* was over. He wanted to take her to England to meet his mother, but the

American authorities refused to issue him with a passport. He contented himself instead with 'goodwill' tours to meet American soldiers. When *Mr Lucky* opened in May 1943, his instinct that it might make a good film was proved triumphantly correct. It rapidly became one of RKO's biggest hits of the year, making a net profit of $1.6 million and a substantial sum for Grant from his profit participation. The critics were less impressed, however. Otis Ferguson dismissed *Mr Lucky* as 'a bad salad with an intelligent dressing' and *Newsweek* added that it was 'as realistic as Hans Christian Andersen and occasionally several times as arch'.

Nevertheless, it was to remain one of Grant's favourite films. 'The character I played was more like the real Cary Grant than any before. *Mr Lucky* was seemingly a happy-go-lucky guy, but that was a cover for a sensitive soul.'

Nowhere was Grant's sensitivity more apparent than at home. The more he sat there doing nothing, the more disconsolate he became. Unable to stand the inactivity, he accepted Jack Warner's offer to make a picture to help the war effort. Warner wanted to make a film about the war in the Pacific, a portrait of life in the American submarines in action there. Delmer Daves, who had been a writer at MGM for ten years and had just joined Warner Brothers, had worked up a story based on a magazine article about an American submarine's trip to Tokyo Bay. The submarine's commander was to be the personification of America's submariners; strong, silent, even a little sad. And Warner wanted Grant. He knew as well as Hitchcock that every member of the audience would sympathize with him as the commander.

Daves had never directed before, but with Grant's support shooting started on 23 June in a specially constructed submarine interior built on the Warners lot. The only difficulty was that Grant had also agreed to start a film for Columbia in the middle of September, which meant that Daves had just six weeks to shoot

DENIED THE OPPORTUNITY TO JOIN THE AMERICAN ARMY AIR CORPS BY THE AMERICAN GOVERNMENT, GRANT SET OFF ON A SERIES OF 'GOODWILL' TOURS TO ENTERTAIN THE TROOPS.

Grant seized the opportunity to play an American submarine commander in *Destination Tokyo* in 1943 for Warner Brothers, as his contribution to the war effort.

the film now called *Destination Tokyo*. He did not manage it. By the time Grant was called to Columbia, the Warners film was only a little over half finished. But *Destination Tokyo* had been specifically designed for a Christmas release — the story even opened with the submarine's crew singing carols and suddenly receiving their orders to sail. The only solution was for Grant to shoot for Columbia during the day, and then go to Warners at night to finish. So throughout September and October 1943 Cary Grant filmed *Destination Tokyo* during the evening, and a new film for Columbia during the day. As a result he saw little or nothing of his new wife. He would return home exhausted, usually to find a dinner party in progress, and would retire to bed rather than join in. The cook would send soup up to his room, and he would look at the two scripts for the following day.

By the end of October, however, *Destination Tokyo* was finished, and he could devote all his energy to Columbia's picture. A thin story, with faint echoes of *Mr Lucky*, it once again called for him to play a glib exploiter who finally achieves redemption. This time he was a down-and-out Broadway producer who discovers a nine-year-old boy who has trained his pet caterpillar to dance to the song 'Yes, Sir, That's My Baby' when he plays it on his mouth

MARRIAGE PROVED A
PROBLEM: GRANT AND
HUTTON SEPARATED BRIEFLY
IN THE AUTUMN OF 1944,
ONLY TO BE RECONCILED IN
1945. IT DID NOT LAST.

organ. Based on a radio play called *My
Client Curly*, it had been retitled *Once
Upon a Time*. The female lead was
played by Janet Blair. Cary Grant did
not enjoy it.

When the picture was finished,
shortly before Christmas, the tension
between Grant and Barbara Hutton
came to the surface. She was planning to
entertain forty people at their house during the week between Christmas and the
New Year, while all he wanted was to
spend the time quietly, recuperating from
the past six months. Barbara seemed
determined to surround herself with people. By the time the holiday was over,
the only real contact between them was
through Lance, who had taken to calling

his new stepfather General. Grant was
devoted to the boy, but on 1 January
1944 Lance was to leave to spend the
next six months with his father. The
thought of being without his stepson
served only to intensify Grant's gloom.

One consolation was the reception
for *Destination Tokyo*. *Newsweek* called
Grant's performance 'one of the sound-
est' of his career, and commented,
'Even movie-goers who have developed
a severe allergy to service pictures
should find *Destination Tokyo* high
among the superior films of the war.'
Bosley Crowther in *The New York
Times* was uncharacteristically
ebullient: 'We don't say it is credible; we
don't even suggest it makes sense. But it
does make a pippin of a picture from a
purely melodramatic point of view.' It
was to become one of Warner Brothers'
biggest financial successes of 1944.

As the silences lengthened at home,
Grant turned for support to the play-

wright Clifford Odets, who had become
almost as close a friend as Randolph
Scott. In the months since Grant had left
their house in Santa Monica, Scott had
been escorting his own heiress, Patricia
Stillman, and was about to marry her, a
marriage which would last the rest of his
life. Odets, on the other hand, was
recently divorced from the actress Luise
Rainer, and had time for Grant. A
former actor, the playwright had come
to Hollywood after writing a series of
left-wing plays for New York's Group
Theatre in the 1930s. Intense and insecure, he had a reputation in Hollywood
for 'saving' screenplays that did not
work and, as a result, Grant suggested
that Odets should work on his next film
for RKO. The studio believed they had
found the perfect project to follow up
the success of *Mr Lucky*. They had paid
$60,000 for the rights to a new novel by
Richard Llewellyn, the author of *How
Green Was My Valley*, which had won
the Oscar for Best Picture in 1941. Set in
London, Llewellyn's new novel was
called *None But the Lonely Heart* and
concerned a Cockney who discovers the
meaning of his own life when he learns
his mother is dying. Grant wanted Odets
to rewrite the part of Ernie Mott specifically for him, even though Llewellyn's
character was just nineteen years old.

The two men sat together for hours
in the first weeks of 1944 talking about
Grant's childhood in Bristol and his
feelings about his own mother. Odets
then did everything he could to bring
those experiences to life in his
screenplay. The only question was who
was to direct the picture. Finally, Grant
suggested that Odets be allowed to do it

himself. He felt sure his friend would bring out the best in the story they had spent so much time discussing. He and Odets then decided that they needed Ethel Barrymore to play Ernie Mott's dying mother, and went to great lengths to induce her to return to Hollywood after eleven years in the theatre. They even persuaded RKO to pay the salaries of her touring theatre company for the six weeks she would be filming. Finally Barrymore, whose elder brother John had died of the effects of alcoholism just eighteen months before, accepted.

Shooting started in March, but Odets did not find the task of directing Cary Grant straightforward. 'His simplicity covers up one of the most complex men I've ever met,' he said afterwards, and as filming got under way he quickly came to realize just how much the part of Ernie Mott meant to his star. Grant questioned, reconsidered and debated every line of dialogue before it was finally accepted. One was of particular importance to him. Ethel Barrymore, as Ma Mott, tells her son, 'Love's not for the poor, son. No time for it.' The echoes of his own life were clear. With Odets's help, Cary Grant had done everything he could to bring Archie Leach to life on the screen.

'I thought the picture showed a successful bit of acting,' Grant was to say years later. 'In many ways the part

WRITER CLIFFORD ODETS SPENT WEEKS WITH GRANT ON THE SCRIPT OF *NONE BUT THE LONELY HEART* IN 1944. AT THEIR REQUEST, THE STUDIO THEN TEMPTED ETHEL BARRYMORE TO BECOME HIS CO-STAR.

seemed to fit my nature better than the light-hearted fellows I was used to playing.' The scene in which Ernie Mott breaks down in tears with his mother remained one of Cary Grant's favourite performances for the rest of his life, because, as he put it, 'I didn't do much of that kind of thing.'

The reception for *Once Upon a Time*, which was released while Odets was shooting *None But the Lonely Heart*, convinced Grant that he had been right to search for a more serious direction. The flimsiness of Columbia's picture showed through. 'There just isn't enough material for a full-length feature,' suggested one critic, while

applauding Grant's 'good characterization'; the *Nation*'s James Agee called it 'not wonderful...just less witty and more gently intentioned than the radio hit' on which it was based.

To be taken seriously Cary Grant knew that he had to do more drama and hoped that *None But the Lonely Heart* would send a signal to Hollywood that he wanted to be thought of as more than simply a wise-cracking leading man in screwball comedies. When filming was completed in June, Grant had his script leather bound and sent to Odets as a present. The playwright wrote back immediately telling him that how proud he should be of his performance: 'Such

reality, constantly moving and warm, I have seldom seen in any film.' Odets finished by comparing his friend to the hero in a Conrad novel, suggesting he shared with Conrad's heroes a 'quality of decency' and goodness 'that comes from the heart'.

Though neither man knew it at the time, *None But the Lonely Heart* was to be the last film Grant made for almost a year. The tensions in his marriage were to keep him away from a sound stage for the next eleven months. But these were not the only cause of his disappearance. There was also the question of custody of Lance Reventlow. The boy's father, who had been taking care of him in New York, suddenly announced in July 1944 that he would not be returning him to California, and instituted legal proceedings alleging that Hutton had 'used coarse and vulgar language in the boy's presence' and had 'sought to undermine his affection for his father'. Count Reventlow's suit also demanded that Cary Grant should never be allowed to speak to the boy.

It was the final straw. As Grant and Hutton started legal proceedings to fight Reventlow's action, so the strain on their relationship grew. Lance had been the one thing holding them together; without him and with every possibility that he might never return, their future together seemed bleak. Eventually, in August, Grant moved out of Westridge and into an apartment in Beverly Hills. Four days later, he tried to persuade Hutton that they should try again, but she refused. Undeterred, he moved back into their house in Pacific Palisades, only to watch her move out. The following

day she told Louella Parsons, 'There is no chance of a reconciliation.'

Grant was convinced his life was ruined. When Jack Warner rang him to say he wanted him to star as Cole Porter in a film biography that Warner Brothers were planning, Grant told the studio boss that there was no point in discussing pictures. Warner pressed him, explaining that Michael Curtiz, the Hungarian who had just won the Oscar for Best Director for *Casablanca*, was going to direct. But Grant was firm. He would not discuss it. Even the reviews for *None But the Lonely Heart*, which was released a few days later, failed to lift his spirits. *Time* called it 'one of the pictures of the year, a feather in the cap of all concerned in its making', and *Variety* dubbed it 'a class picture'. Grant's own work was particularly singled out for praise. In *The New York Times* Bosley Crowther described his performance as 'an exceptional characterization of bewilderment and arrogance', while the *Hollywood Reporter* called it simply the 'finest thing he has ever done'.

By a strange irony, *Arsenic and Old Lace* was released the following day to almost equally enthusiastic reviews. The film

NO FILM IN HIS CAREER MEANT MORE THAN *NONE BUT THE LONELY HEART*: THE STORY OF A COCKNEY WHO DISCOVERS THE MEANING OF LIFE WHEN HIS MOTHER, PLAYED BY ETHEL BARRYMORE, IS DYING.

had been sitting on the Warner Brothers shelves for more than two years, but Ida Lupino enthused in the *Saturday Evening Post*, 'I was helpless with laughter as I watched Cary change from a normal young man to a decidedly dizzy one, talking to himself, staring into the window seat from which bodies mysteriously appeared and disappeared, and making various wild attempts to cope with the situation.' Howard Barnes in the *New York Herald Tribune*, however, came closer to Grant's own view: 'For

some reason or other, a fine actor merely mugs through the part of the sane member of the Brewster clan.'

Cary Grant did not take any interest in the reviews for either film. He was preoccupied with planning one last attempt at a reconciliation with Barbara Hutton. He had decided to drive up to see her in San Francisco. When he arrived, she agreed to see him and they spent the last weekend of September 1944 together discussing their future. Within a few days they were back

together — in a new house in Bellagio Road overlooking the Bel Air golf course, not large enough to accommodate Hutton's servants or her companion. A delighted Grant instructed the RKO publicity department to issue a brief statement confirming their reconciliation, and then he and his wife disappeared. He had promised Barbara he would spend more time with her.

For a time they became 'millionaire recluses', in the words of one gossip column. Hutton tried to accept that he

could not stand her dinner parties — where everyone seemed 'only ever to speak in French' — and tried to share his fascination with whose film had 'opened well'. But they were still uncomfortable with each other, conscious that each was trying too hard. Gradually his dark moods began to return, and she became more remote. Finally, five months after their reconciliation, Hutton and Grant accepted the inevitable. On 26 February 1945 she moved out of the house on Bellagio Road and back to Westridge in Pacific Palisades. They issued a brief statement: 'After much thought and with great consideration we have decided we can be happier living apart. As yet no formal plans have been formed regarding divorce.' The next day Louella Parsons was predicting confidently that Hutton would leave Hollywood, 'for since her reconciliation with Cary not one of her friends has seen her... They have been in complete seclusion.'

For the next few months, Cary Grant remained in that seclusion. The failure of his second marriage seemed to overwhelm him. Certainly the seventeenth Academy Awards did nothing to alleviate his despair. Though he had been nominated for an Oscar as Best Actor for his performance as Ernie Mott in *None But the Lonely Heart*, the award went to Bing Crosby for *Going My Way*. The fact that Ethel Barrymore won as Best Supporting Actress merely sharpened Grant's sense of isolation, the feeling that he was doomed never to be taken seriously as an actor. For the next eight weeks, Cary Grant hardly went out and barely talked to a soul.

CHAPTER FIVE • NOTORIOUS

Finally, on 12 May 1945, Grant ended his self-imposed exile and reported to Warner Brothers to start work on their long-delayed biography of Cole Porter. Jack Warner had persuaded him that he could not sit at home managing his investments for the rest of his life. But when he arrived at the studio, he wondered whether he had been wise. The shooting script of *Night and Day*, as the film was to be called, was a mess. Four writers had already worked on it and there had been so many drafts that Michael Curtiz had a large cardboard box in his room filled with pages from the various versions.

Grant directed all the pain and frustration that had been building up in him over the past year towards the script. On the third day of shooting the unit manager noted that he 'complained all day long yesterday about the dialogue — how bad it was, how poorly written — and what lousy characterization it gave him'. Two months later he reported, 'Mike is just about frantic with all this rewriting (for your information it comes mostly from Cary Grant picking at and criticizing the script).' By the end of three months, Curtiz was threatening to walk off the set altogether, because Grant seemed to want 'to direct it himself'. The crew joked that the Americans should have dropped their atomic bomb on Warners rather than Hiroshima: 'That's the only way the war between the director and the star will ever come to an end.'

One reason for Cary Grant's anxiety was that he knew Cole Porter personally and was concerned that the film did not convey either his friend's 'extraordinary talent' or 'the graciousness of its possessor'. (In fact Porter, who had been paid $300,000 for the rights to his songs and had been particularly keen that Grant should play him on the screen, had no complaints about his portrayal.) The other reason for Grant's irritability on the set, of course, had nothing to do with the life story of Cole Porter, and everything to do with his own life. Eight weeks after shooting began Barbara Hutton filed for divorce in the Los Angeles Superior Court. The grounds she chose were 'mental cruelty'.

At the end of August, while Grant was filming *Night and Day*, Hutton appeared in court. She claimed that her husband had caused her 'great mental anguish' because he had often refused to

'You don't lose your identity up on the screen. It's always you, no matter how you behave... It's much more difficult than anyone could possibly imagine.'

BACK AT WORK AFTER THE COLLAPSE OF HIS SECOND MARRIAGE, GRANT STARRED OPPOSITE ALEXIS SMITH IN *NIGHT AND DAY* (ABOVE RIGHT), THEN TEAMED WITH HITCHCOCK TO MAKE *NOTORIOUS* WITH INGRID BERGMAN (LEFT).

AN ENORMOUS HIT AT THE
BOX OFFICE IN 1946, NIGHT
AND DAY NEVERTHELESS DID
NOT APPEAL TO THE CRITICS.
ONE DESCRIBED HIM AS 'SO
UNDERPLAYING THE ROLE THAT
HE'S ALWAYS CARY GRANT'.

come downstairs when she gave a dinner
party, and 'when he did come down he
was obviously not amused'. The entire
hearing lasted four minutes. As *Time*
magazine remarked, 'She would have
made it in three if she had not taken
time out to pose for the photographers.'
Grant did not defend himself, nor did he
accept any financial settlement from his
wife. He remained absolutely silent as
Hutton was awarded a divorce. As a
result he was to remain one of Hutton's
few friends until her death in May 1979,
as well as unofficial guardian to his
stepson, Lance Reventlow, who was to
die in an air crash in 1972, at the age of
thirty-six.

Grant's divorce did not end the
arguments with Curtiz, however. On the
final day of shooting in mid-October, he
even told the director, 'If I'm chump
enough ever to be caught working for
you again, you'll know I'm either broke
or I've lost my mind.' He was convinced
that the film would be a complete
failure.

He could not have been more
wrong. *Night and Day* was to become
one of the studio's biggest hits when it
was released in July 1946, even though
Life magazine called it 'a remarkably
complete dossier of all that is wrong
with the current musical film'. After the
première, Grant sent Curtiz a telegram
of apology. A week after finishing *Night
and Day*, Grant was back at RKO.

ONCE AGAIN HITCHCOCK
BROUGHT OUT HIS MENACE
IN *NOTORIOUS*, BUT IT WAS
THE ADDITION OF INGRID
BERGMAN, HERE WITH
GRANT AND HITCHCOCK OFF
THE SET, THAT ADDED AN
EXTRA, SENSUAL, QUALITY.

Alfred Hitchcock had offered him the
part of Devlin, a mysterious United
States government agent who falls in
love with a young woman who marries
someone else for the good of her
adopted country, in a new film to be
called *Notorious*. Hitchcock had always
wanted to make a film about a man in
love with a woman who is forced,
because of her official duties, to go to
bed with another man, and the project
had originally been prepared for
David O. Selznick. But RKO had
picked it up for $800,000, together with
Hitchcock, the writer Ben Hecht and
the young woman who was to be its
female star, Ingrid Bergman.

From the moment they were
introduced, Grant was entranced by
Bergman. He liked the fact that she did
not wear make-up or expensive clothes,
and that she took acting seriously. And
as the filming got under way, Bergman
encouraged him to relax. On the screen
the luminous star of *Casablanca* seemed
to shine even more brightly alongside
Grant's cool, dark elegance. Grant
meanwhile seemed more attractive than
he had ever been, calmer and more
certain of himself, and he gave a
performance that perfectly displayed
his capacity for menacing charm.

Nowhere was the sexual electricity
between them more apparent than in the
scene in which they kissed for the first

FATEFUL FASCINATION! ELECTRIC TENSION!

The screen's top romantic stars in a melodramatic masterpiece!

CARY GRANT · INGRID BERGMAN

Adventurous Man! *Notorious Woman!*

in ALFRED HITCHCOCK'S

NOTORIOUS!

Directed by ALFRED HITCHCOCK Written by BEN HECHT SRO

CLAUDE RAINS
LOUIS CALHERN

NOTORIOUS IN 1946 PROVED THAT GRANT HAD BECOME ONE OF THE CINEMA'S GREAT STARS. THE STUDIO PUBLICITY STILLS OF THE PERIOD (*LEFT*) REFLECTED HIS EXTRA CONFIDENCE.

time. The American Production Code insisted that no screen kiss should last for longer than three seconds, but Hitchcock, Bergman and Grant overcame it. As Bergman put it later, 'We just kissed each other and talked, leaned away and kissed each other again. Then the telephone came between us, and then we moved to the other side of the telephone. So it was a kiss which opened and closed: but the censors couldn't and didn't cut the scene because we never at any point kissed for more than three seconds. We did other things, we nibbled each other's ears and kissed a cheek so that it looked endless, and it became sensational in Hollywood.'

Cary Grant's performance in *Notorious* underlined how far his unique qualities as a screen actor had matured in the years since *The Awful Truth*. He had become more careful and restrained than the eyebrow-arching Jerry Warriner; he was now a man who had been hurt but who had survived, wounded but wiser. When the film opened at the Radio City Music Hall in July 1946, the critics paid fulsome tribute. In *The New York Times*, Bosley Crowther called *Notorious* a 'romantic melodrama which is just about as thrilling as they come — velvet smooth in dramatic action, sharp and sure in its characters and heavily charged with the intensity of warm emotional appeal'. Crowther, along with almost every other critic, also noticed that Hitchcock had made Bergman the seductress and Grant the man to be pursued. Alfred Hitchcock

In the kissing sequence in *Notorious* Hitchcock's stars flouted the production code by kissing passionately, but intermittently, for much longer than the code allowed.

had thereby forged the final, decisive part of Cary Grant's screen persona.

Shortly after filming was over Grant set off for his first visit to England since the end of the war. The United States government was now prepared to give him a passport, and he wanted to celebrate his mother's sixty-ninth birthday with her in Bristol. But when he saw her for the first time in five years, Grant realized nothing had changed. The small wiry woman was still as fiercely independent as she had been ever since she re-entered his life, and she still managed to make him feel uncomfortable. He would sit with her and she would tell him how pleased she was to see him, and yet he could never quite escape the feeling that nothing he did would ever truly please her, and that when she complimented him he did not really deserve it.

Like *Night and Day*, *Notorious* was to become one of the biggest box-office successes of 1946, making RKO a profit of more than $1 million. By the time it was released Grant was filming again. His self-imposed exile after Barbara Hutton's departure was firmly in the past. Shortly after his return from Engand in June, he started work for the studio again, this time starring opposite Myrna Loy and the seventeen-year-old Shirley Temple in a project which had started life as an original screenplay by a twenty-nine-year-old former script reader called Sidney Sheldon. The original title was *Too Good to Be True*,

SHIRLEY TEMPLE WAS THE
LATEST WOMAN TO PURSUE
GRANT ON THE SCREEN.
WITH HIS HELP, SHE BECAME
A BELIEVABLE TEENAGER IN
*THE BACHELOR AND THE
BOBBYSOXER* IN 1947.

but the film's producer, Dore Schary, had renamed it *The Bachelor and the Bobby Soxer*. Designed to establish Temple as a believable teenager on the screen, it demanded that the former child star should subject Grant to a bewildering array of teenage activities, including eating ice-cream sodas and doing the jitterbug, while her elder sister, played by Loy, looked on.

Throughout the shooting Grant fussed, as he had done so often before, but he also allowed Temple to control the screen. By delicately underplaying his own role, he enabled the young woman to blossom, and when the film was released in September 1947 *Variety* paid tribute to his 'expert timing', which, it added, 'proves a terrific lift to an occasionally awkward plot'. The film was to become his fifth consecutive hit, bringing RKO more than $5 million in film rentals from the United States alone. It was also to win Sidney Sheldon an Academy Award for his screenplay.

In public, Cary Grant still liked to preserve the image that he had so carefully constructed on the screen. He certainly did not care to reveal his private insecurities to the cinema audience, and this made him particularly cautious about accepting any role that might hint he was not what he appeared to be. Alfred Hitchcock had suggested that he would make a perfect Hamlet on film,

and had even commissioned a screenplay, but Grant had politely declined. Harry Cohn at Columbia had tried to persuade him to play the lead in Ruth Gordon and Garson Kanin's new script, *A Double Life*, about an actor playing Othello who becomes so obsessed with his role that he murders the actress playing Desdemona. But, once again, Grant turned the part down. It might have been a mistake, as the role was to win an Oscar for Ronald Colman.

Insecurity about revealing too much

about himself was not the only limitation to the parts Cary Grant would consider playing. There was also the question of his fee. Money had become one certain means of stilling the private fears that still plagued him, and he had become expert at the business of making movies. Together with his agent Frank Vincent, he had managed to obtain for himself some of the best profit participations of any actor working in Hollywood. Some of his friends even suspected that he enjoyed the process of making the deal more than the performances themselves, although he denied it.

Sam Goldwyn was certainly aware of Cary Grant's reputation as a business-man. But the Polish-born producer of such hits as *Wuthering Heights* and *The Pride of the Yankees* also knew Grant's value at the box-office, and he needed him to guarantee another winner. Goldwyn wanted to follow the success of RKO's films about the life of a young Catholic priest, *Going My Way* and *The Bells of St Mary's*, with a religious comedy of his own, although it was to

be a Protestant one, based on Robert Nathan's novel *The Bishop's Wife*. Grant was to play a bishop so obsessed with raising money for a new cathedral that he drifts apart from his wife, to be played by Loretta Young, only to find himself assisted by Dudley, an angel in human form, to be played by David Niven. The script had been written by Robert Sherwood, who had just won an Oscar for *The Best Years of Our Lives* for Goldwyn, and revised by Leonardo Bercovici. Cary Grant negotiated his deal himself. It guaranteed him a minimum of $300,000.

On 1 February 1947 Grant arrived at RKO to start work. The director of *The Bishop's Wife* was William Seiter, a former Keystone Cop who had become one of Hollywood's most accomplished crafts-men with light comedy, but the rehearsals did not go well. Once again, Grant fretted that he could not make his role work, while Goldwyn did not like the approach Seiter was taking. David Niven was struggling to come to terms with the sudden tragic death of his first wife, Primula, only a

few weeks before. Finally, after the first weeks of shooting, Goldwyn decided to change the director. Seiter was paid his full fee, but replaced by Henry Koster, who had been directing in Hollywood since the Thirties. Nor did Goldwyn stop there. He also insisted that Grant and Niven swop roles, making Grant the angel and Niven the bishop. The decision infuriated Grant, who felt he understood the 'befuddled' cleric and said so. In retaliation Goldwyn fined him, only to reinstate the payment once filming had restarted.

No matter how fraught the filming had been, when *The Bishop's Wife* was released to catch the 1947 Christmas audience — not least because it featured a Christmas Eve reconciliation between the bishop and his wife — it appealed to the critics. *The New York Times* called it 'as cheerful an invasion of the realm of conscience as we have seen', while *Variety* described it as 'fluent and beguiling' as Cary Grant 'rescues the role from the ultimate peril of coyness'. It did not, however, quite match the appeal of *The Bachelor and the Bobbysoxer* at the box-office.

In August 1947, as soon as shooting on *The Bishop's Wife* was over, Grant once again left Hollywood for England. He had two months free before he was due to embark on another film, and that presented a chance to see his mother. This time he made the journey in the company of a friend, the English play-wright Frederick Lonsdale, author of *The Last of Mrs Cheyney*. After Grant had paid his customary visit to Bristol, he and Lonsdale went to the theatre together in London, and in late

AS SOON AS HE HAD FINISHED *THE BISHOP'S WIFE* FOR SAMUEL GOLDWYN IN 1947, ALONGSIDE DAVID NIVEN (RIGHT), GRANT RETURNED TO ENGLAND TO VISIT HIS MOTHER IN BRISTOL (LEFT).

LEFT AND ABOVE: IN *THE
BISHOP'S WIFE* GRANT
PLAYED A 'BLITHE SPIRIT' WHO
MATERIALIZES TO ANSWER A
YOUNG BISHOP'S PRAYERS,
AND HELPS SAVE BOTH
CHURCH AND HIS MARRIAGE
AT CHRISTMAS.

September set off back across the
Atlantic on the *Queen Elizabeth*. On
board ship Grant noticed a twenty-
four-year-old actress they had seen in
London in a play called *Deep Are the
Roots*. Her name was Betsy Drake.

After arranging an introduction,
Grant ate every meal during the five-day
voyage with the young actress, the
daughter of a writer, born in Paris in
1923. Brought up in Washington, Drake

had become a model, then an actress in
New York, before accepting an
invitation from H.M. Tennent to
appear on Shaftesbury Avenue. 'She
intrigued me no end,' Grant confessed.
'She was interested in astronomy and
yoga — subjects I'd never investigated
myself — and she was bookish, but
charmingly so.' By the time they reached
New York, Betsy Drake had become
Grant's latest project. He was determined
to help her become a star in Hollywood.

Drake herself was sceptical, but
Grant persisted, telling her repeatedly
that she could have a part in one of his
films. After a time, she politely accepted
his invitation to join him in California.
There was no job waiting for her in New

York, and Hollywood might have
something to offer. But she refused to be
seen as the latest 'friend' of a famous
star. Drake insisted that she find her
own apartment, and go to her own
auditions. She might still stammer when
she was nervous, but her father's
family had built the famous Drake Hotel
in Chicago, and she did not intend to be
taken for granted.

As Grant arrived to start work on
his new film for RKO in October 1947,
where Dore Schary was now in charge
of production and David O. Selznick
was his producer, Betsy Drake settled
herself into a small apartment in
Hollywood. Grant introduced her to the
agent Ray Stark, who was eventually to

After years of nervous-
ness on the set, Grant
seemed to relax on *Mr
Blandings Builds His
Dream House*, with Myrna
Loy, in 1948. 'It was a
joy,' he said later.

represent her, as well as to both Schary
and Selznick, and he coached her for the
screen test that RKO had offered her. He
made no secret of the fact that he
wanted her to be his co-star, and RKO
were not anxious to upset the man
who had made nine box-office hits for
them over the past ten years. After the
test, Schary and Selznick offered Betsy
Drake a contract between them, and
agreed to consider her for the picture
after the one that Grant was just about
to start shooting.

Satisfied, Grant started work on *Mr
Blandings Builds His Dream House*, a
comedy based on the simple idea that
every successful New York advertising
executive longs to escape his cramped
Manhattan apartment for a house in
Connecticut. Grant was to play the
advertising executive Jim Blandings and
Myrna Loy his wife Muriel. Written by
Norman Panama and Melvin Frank
from an Eric Hodgins novel, the film
was to be directed by Hank Potter, who
had last worked with Grant on *Mr
Lucky*. This time, in place of a dancing
caterpillar, Potter was to have a
clapboard country house that seemed
destined never to be completed. 'I loved
it,' Potter recalled years later. 'The film
was a pleasure to make.' Myrna Loy
agreed, and even Dore Schary noticed
that Grant's customary fidgety

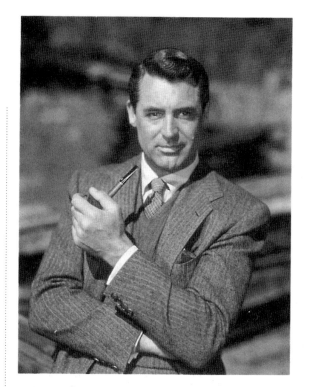

THE STORY OF AN ADVERTISING MAN INTENT ON ESCAPING FROM MANHATTAN TO CONNECTICUT, *MR BLANDINGS* REMAINS A FAVOURITE OF NEW YORKERS TODAY.

Crosby, *Every Girl Should Be Married* was exactly the sort of comedy that Grant's audience expected of him. He was to play a successful paediatrician, Dr Madison Brown, who has meticulously protected his bachelor status until a young saleswoman in the children's department of a local store, to be played by Drake, mounts an elaborate campaign to capture him. He had taken a hand in polishing the script, along with Hartman and his collaborator Stephen Morehouse Avery, and there was an echo of his romance with Drake in the story. Like his film character, Grant wanted to be wanted by an independent young woman.

Whatever the underlying emotions, the cinema audience loved the picture. *Every Girl Should Be Married* turned out to be RKO's biggest box-office success of the year when it was released in December 1948, making more than $750,000 in profits for the studio. The critics, on the other hand, loathed it. *Newsweek* suggested it was 'a light-headed little comedy' which believed that 'eligible bachelors are unsocial creatures who like to shut themselves up in fusty rooms full of stuffed fish and moose antlers' and dismissed it as 'contrived and overcute'. *Time* agreed: 'Newcomer Betsy Drake seems to have studied, but not learned, the tricks and inflections of the early Hepburn. Her exaggerated grimaces supply only one solid laugh —

uncertainty had waned a little under the influence of Betsy Drake.

The good nature that surrounded the production was reflected in the reviews. When *Mr Blandings Builds His Dream House* opened in March 1948, the *New Yorker* said it had 'all the standard ingredients, from the closet in the hall which disgorges everything in it when the door is opened to the springs in the cellar that rise like the Mississippi without warning'. The critic James Agee added, 'A bulls-eye for middle-class middlebrows.'

By that time, Cary Grant had got his way. RKO had confirmed that Betsy Drake was to be his next co-star. And in late May, they started work together. Written, produced and directed by Don Hartman, who had written three of the *Road* films for Bob Hope and Bing

DORE SCHARY Presents

CARY GRANT · MYRNA LOY · MELVYN DOUGLAS

MR. BLANDINGS BUILDS HIS DREAM HOUSE

REGINALD DENNY SHARYN MOFFETT CONNIE MARSHALL LOUISE BEAVERS IAN WOLFE
Produced and written for the Screen by NORMAN PANAMA and MELVIN FRANK
Directed by H. C. POTTER · An RKO Radio Production · A Selznick Release

when hero Grant mimics them cruelly and accurately. In the past, Cary Grant has shown a talent for quietly underplaying comedy. In the picture, he has trouble finding comedy to play.'

After fifty-two films in just sixteen years, Cary Grant was established as one of Hollywood's biggest stars. In the past year alone he had earned more than $350,000 from his pictures, together with substantial profits from earlier successes. To confirm it, *Fame* magazine had just named him one of the industry's top ten actors, alongside Gary Cooper, Humphrey Bogart, Clark Gable and Spencer Tracy. Now he wanted to exploit his position by selling his talents to the highest bidder. Even though RKO was now owned by his old friend Howard Hughes, *Every Girl Should Be Married* was the last film that Grant was to make for the studio.

Grant wanted fresh and richer pastures, but not fresh collaborators. He still preferred to work with people he knew and trusted. So the first picture he made away from RKO was for Howard Hawks. They had not worked together since *His Girl Friday*, but Hawks had sensed that Grant might like the opportunity to make a comedy in Europe, away from the American critics, and had suggested an idea to him. The story Hawks had in mind focused on a French army officer newly married to a female American officer. Prevented from consummating his marriage by her army commitments, he decides to dress up as a female officer to circumvent regulations. With a script by Charles Lederer, who had written *His Girl Friday*, together with Leonard

Spigelglass and Hagar Wilde, and based on a story by Henri Rochard, the film was to be called *I Was a Male War Bride*. Hawks thought the idea of spending a good proportion of a film dressed up as a woman might appeal to Grant's appetite for pantomime.

IN 1948 GRANT PERSUADED RKO TO USE BETSY DRAKE, A YOUNG WOMAN HE HAD MET ON AN ATLANTIC CROSSING, AS HIS CO-STAR IN *EVERY GIRL SHOULD BE MARRIED*. SHE BECAME HIS THIRD WIFE.

LEFT: HOWARD HAWKS
BROUGHT OUT THE UNEXPECTED
SIDE OF HIS STAR IN *I Was a
Male War Bride* IN 1949.
GRANT SPENT MOST OF THE
PICTURE DRESSED AS A
WOMAN, WEARING A
RIDICULOUS WIG (*RIGHT*).

Before the project got under way, *I Was a Male War Bride* promised to be as successful as *His Girl Friday*, but not everything went according to plan. No sooner had Cary Grant arrived in Germany to start work in September 1948 than bad weather stopped production. Then his co-star Ann Sheridan caught pleurisy, which turned into pneumonia, and another crew member came down with jaundice. Grant was certain the production was jinxed. Within a few days, he had been taken ill with hepatitis and been transported to London, where a British doctor ordered him to stay in bed and rest. As Christmas approached Grant grew gradually weaker and weaker. It was as if he had lost the will to recover.

Betsy Drake saved him. As he admitted later, 'She nursed me back to health.' It was a revelation to him. The young actress's obvious concern for his health convinced him that he had at last found a woman who would give him the unquestioning affection that he had craved ever since his mother's disappearance. Drake seemed to want nothing more than to make his life the most important thing in her own. By the end of February 1949, when he was well enough to travel, they decided to take a long sea voyage back to Los Angeles, to give him time to recuperate. On the voyage, Cary Grant asked Betsy Drake to marry him.

She refused to consider marriage for the moment. 'If I should marry before I have at least two successful pictures,' she later explained to the columnist Louella Parsons, 'no matter how good I might be, I would simply be known as Mrs Cary Grant.'

Hawks finished *I Was a Male War Bride* in the early spring of 1949, and as soon as the filming was over Cary Grant checked himself into the John Hopkins Hospital in Baltimore for a complete physical examination. But now, after waiting more than a year, Twentieth Century Fox were anxious to release the picture as quickly as possible, and the studio shipped the first prints to the cinemas for release in the first week of September. Though Bosley Crowther noted in *The New York Times* that 'the flimsiness of the film's foundations and the disorder of its episodes provoke the inevitable impression that it all fell together en route', *Newsweek* called it 'one of the most sparkingly original comedies of the year'. It was to become another box-office triumph.

Grant's illness had taken its toll, however, and he did not feel well enough to make another film during 1949. Instead, he and Betsy appeared in a radio version of *Every Girl Should Be Married* for the Lux Theatre on CBS, and he made another appearance on the show with Shirley Temple in a radio version of *The Bachelor and the Bobbysoxer*. Radio was all that he would agree to — he was determined to take the rest of the year off to recover completely. He was also trying to persuade Betsy to become his wife.

In the end Howard Hughes

IN *CRISIS* (LEFT), GRANT
PLAYED A BRAIN SURGEON.
FILMING STARTED JUST DAYS
AFTER HIS THIRD MARRIAGE,
TO BETSY DRAKE, SEEN HERE
WITH DIRECTOR RICHARD
BROOKS (ABOVE).

intervened. On Christmas Day 1949, he picked Grant and Drake up from Beverly Hills, drove them to Glendale Airport, north of Hollywood, put them into one of his own planes and flew them to Phoenix in Arizona. He had decided the time had come for them to get married, and they had agreed. Hughes was the best man at the five-minute ceremony. The bride was twenty-six and the groom almost forty-six. As a wedding gift he presented her with a string of pearls with a diamond clasp, along with a poodle named Suzie. There was no time for a honeymoon. Grant was to start a new film for MGM on 1 January 1950.

Dore Schary had left RKO the previous year to become production chief at MGM and he wanted to make a political thriller written by a young reporter turned screenwriter called Richard Brooks. A few years before, Brooks had collaborated with John Huston to write *Key Largo* for Humphrey Bogart, and now he wanted to direct himself. The story of a brain surgeon whose wife is kidnapped while on holiday in South America and who is therefore blackmailed into operating secretly on an ailing dictator, the film was to be called *Crisis*. Grant was to play the surgeon, with José Ferrer as the dictator, and Grant suggested that Brooks hire three silent stars for three Spanish-speaking roles: Ramon Navarro, the original Ben Hur, Gilbert Roland and Antonio Moreno. The only other stipulation was that shooting would take just

thirty-six days. Brooks made sure that it did — after all, Cary Grant had given him the chance to direct.

As soon as *Crisis* was over, Grant retired to his house in Palm Springs. He remembered only too well the mistakes he had made the last time, spending day after day at the studio while Barbara Hutton languished at home. He did not intend to repeat them. Throughout the rest of 1950, he was hardly in Hollywood. He took Betsy to see his

BETSY DRAKE WROTE A
RADIO SERIES, WHICH SHE
RECORDED WITH HER NEW
HUSBAND IN 1950.

mother in England, and made a radio series from *Mr Blandings Builds His Dream House*, which Betsy had written. He turned down an approach from David O. Selznick to make a film version of F. Scott Fitzgerald's Hollywood story *Tender Is the Night*, and another from Howard Hughes to make a film version of Terence Rattigan's play *O Mistress Mine*, which had been a hit on Broadway for the Lunts. Betsy Drake introduced him to new kinds of music and diets, explaining the benefits of hypnotism and meditation, and he seemed quite content to let her do so. When *Crisis* was released on 4 July, he and his new wife barely noticed. In fact, the critics were admiring. The *Los Angeles Mirror* commented, '*Crisis* is a bold piece of movie adventuring.... Cary

Grant is more brittle and diamond-brilliant than before as the enlightened doctor. His sincerity in the story's guts is its premise for being believed.' Unfortunately the audiences did not agree. *Crisis* became Grant's first box-office failure in almost a decade.

It was Joe Mankiewicz, the young producer who had worked with him on *The Philadelphia Story*, who finally tempted Cary Grant back to work again. In the past two years Mankiewicz had become the most successful director and screenwriter in Hollywood. He had won the Oscar for Best Director and Best Screenwriter for *A Letter to Three Wives* and was about to win the same two Oscars again for *All About Eve*. Enthusiastic, intelligent and with a spectacular talent for crisp, often sarcastic dialogue, Mankiewicz wanted nothing more than to make a new film with Cary Grant. And Darryl Zanuck at Fox wanted nothing more than to cash in on the writer and director who had just won the studio a clutch of Oscars. If Mankiewicz wanted to make a film version of Kurt Goetz's Broadway comedy-drama, *Dr Praetorius*, about a crusading doctor who marries a pregnant but unmarried girl who has just tried to commit suicide, that was fine with Zanuck. If Mankiewicz could also persuade Grant to play the doctor, all the better. Zanuck was even prepared to guarantee Grant $300,000. In the end, Mankiewicz, the fee and the script proved an offer that Grant could not afford to refuse.

When filming started in the early spring of 1951, Fox were so confident of success that they organized a rapid

release for *People Will Talk*, as Mankiewicz had renamed the play, with a spectacular Los Angeles première in July. But, though Grant took elaborate professional advice from a leading heart surgeon and insisted that the sets be as authentic as possible, Mankiewicz did not work the same magic again. *People Will Talk* did not do for Cary Grant what *All About Eve* had done for George Sanders: it did not win him an Oscar, although it did bring him respectful reviews. *Newsweek* suggested he gave 'one of the most intelligent performances in his nineteen-year Hollywood career'. *The New York Times* called it 'a significant milestone in the moral emancipation of American films' and complimented Grant on 'the delightfulness and good sense of his performance'. The only drawback was that the cinema audience did not like it. The film became Grant's second successive flop, and one of the four films he disliked the most in his career.

In the wake of his second failure, Cary Grant decided that it might be wiser to work with his wife again — perhaps that way he could repeat the success of *Every Girl Should Be Married*. Warners had come up with a script for them both, called *Room for One More*, and he was to be guaranteed 10 per cent of the gross receipts, with a minimum of $100,000, while Betsy was to be paid $25,000. Warners were also only too happy to give him the special dressing room that he liked, and to accept that he wanted to finish the picture quickly. After discussing it with Betsy, Grant agreed.

The story of a city engineer whose

wife likes to look after unwanted children as well as her own, and based on a best-selling novel by Anna Perrott Rose, *Room for One More* was a gentle domestic comedy written by Jack Rose and Mel Shavelson. It certainly appealed to Betsy Drake, who wanted nothing more than to create her own new family and did not mind at all if the cinema audience began to see Cary Grant as a husband and father rather than the eligible bachelor of the past. As filming began in July 1951, with Norman Taurog as director, Grant told reporters, 'Domesticity is a great invention, more people should relax and enjoy it.' For her part, Drake told an interviewer, 'We don't always see as much of our friends as we should, but the truth of the matter is that we seldom entertain.' The five children by whom they found themselves surrounded on set provided a surrogate family. Grant and Drake gave each of their screen children a present, and made home movies of them.

Warners were so pleased with *Room for One More* that they rushed it out just after the turn of the year. The *Hollywood Reporter* called it 'a delightful domestic comedy' and described Grant's performance as ''witty, debonair, but always real'.

Variety praised the film for being 'happy', and *Time* magazine admitted, 'The movie's handling of child behaviour is unusually sound for a Hollywood film, fairly free of obvious tear-jerking.' As the film opened it looked as though it would be as big a hit as *Every Girl Should Be Married*.

But the audience, and the cinema itself, had changed in the three years since Cary Grant and Betsy Drake had last appeared together. Television had begun to make its presence felt in America's living rooms, and with it had come lower box-office takings in the cinemas. The studios too had found

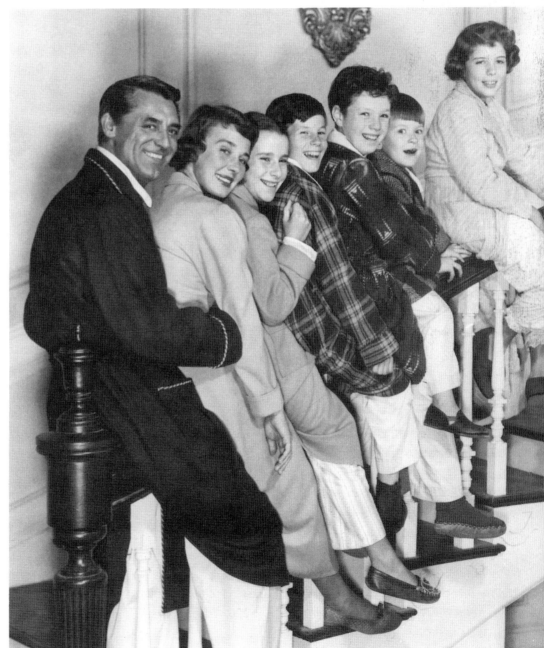

ROOM FOR ONE MORE IN 1952 WAS GRANT'S SECOND FILM WITH BETSY DRAKE. IT PROVIDED THEM WITH THE FAMILY THEY TOLD FRIENDS THEY LONGED FOR.

Above: Ginger Rogers was Grant's co-star in *Monkey Business*, his fifth film for Howard Hawks, but it was the young Marilyn Monroe (*right*) who caught the eye of the critics.

Be Married had been for RKO in 1949.

A slightly perplexed Grant went back to Fox, to work with Howard Hawks for the fifth time. Once again Charles Lederer had written a screenplay, this time in collaboration with Ben Hecht and I.A.L. Diamond, called *Monkey Business*. The idea was straightforward. An absent-minded research chemist, to be played by Grant, accidentally discovers a formula for reversing the ageing process, and a chimpanzee with which he is working pours the formula into the laboratory's water cooler. When the chemist takes a drink he becomes an adolescent, and when his wife, to be played by Ginger Rogers, takes several drinks she begins to act like a child. Marilyn Monroe was to play the secretary who

themselves under threat. In 1949, the United States government had forced them to divest themselves of their chains of cinemas, in what was known as the Paramount decree, with the result that the studios could no longer be sure of as wide and significant a release for all their films. On top of that Hollywood was uncertain what made a box-office success. Now even Cary Grant did not seem to guarantee a hit. *Room for One More* was nothing like as successful for Warners in 1952 as *Every Girl Should*

helps the chemist rediscover his youth on the roller-skating rink.

Grant was not particularly impressed by Monroe. 'I had no idea she would become a big star,' he said later. 'If she had something different from any other actress, it wasn't apparent at the time.' Grant felt she was ambitious, and a little calculating, but he could not fault her professionalism. Nevertheless, he preferred working with the other male lead in the picture, the veteran comedian Charles Coburn. 'I learned how to steal a scene from Charles,' Grant said afterwards. 'He has screwed up more scenes for leading men than I would care to name.' Typically, Coburn had taken care to see that he got one of the funniest lines in the picture, when he told Monroe, as his secretary, 'Find someone to type this.'

There were echoes of *Bringing Up Baby* in *Monkey Business*. This time Grant was a chemist rather than a palaeontologist, and there was a chimpanzee called Peggy rather than a leopard called Nissa, but he again had to call upon his comic timing and his ability as an acrobat, just as he had opposite Hepburn fifteen years before. But by now the worldly character the cinema audience had come to know as Cary Grant did not look quite right as a befuddled scientist. Too many years, and too many Cary Grant pictures, had intervened. After the film was completed, Hawks himself was prepared to admit, 'I don't think the premise of the film was really believable and for that reason it was not as funny as it should have been.'

The critics agreed. 'If youth is anything like the nonsense displayed here,' the *New Yorker* noted, 'maybe it's just as well that nobody has really concocted anything that would force us older citizens back into it.' Bosley Crowther in *The New York Times* added that it was a curiously old-fashioned picture, a 'screwball comedy' now strangely out of place. The year's Oscars went to Vivien Leigh and Karl Malden for *A Streetcar Named Desire,* and to Humphrey Bogart for *The African Queen.* Cary Grant's brand of light romantic comedy no longer seemed to be what the audience wanted.

But there were still tempting offers. At MGM, Dore Schary was keen to repeat the success of *The Bachelor and the Bobbysoxer,* and had asked Sidney Sheldon to write another screenplay specially for Grant. Sheldon and Schary had also misread the times, however. They too were assuming that Cary Grant alone could make an old-fashioned comedy work. *Dream Wife*, as the new film was called, was nothing more than a bit of fluff. The story of an executive who leaves his busy and successful wife for a sheikh's daughter practised in the art of pleasing men, it had been created by Alfred Lewis Levitt, who had worked with Sheldon and Herbert Baker on the screenplay. But not even Deborah Kerr, who had recently been nominated for an Oscar for *Edward My Son* and was about to win with *From Here to Eternity,* could make the film feel contemporary. It was a relic from an earlier Hollywood age. When *Dream Wife* appeared in June 1953, the *Hollywood Reporter* dismissed it as 'stretched out far beyond the value of

DREAM WIFE WAS CREATED SPECIALLY FOR GRANT BY SIDNEY SHELDON (RIGHT), BUT NOT EVEN THE SKILL OF HIS CO-STAR DEBORAH KERR COULD QUITE SAVE IT FROM THE CRITICS.

its basic premise', while *Newsweek* called it 'an uneven mixture of sophisticated humour and downright slapstick moments' which amounted to 'little more than fairly amusing comedy'.

Realistic drama had taken the place of romantic comedy. The dinner jacket and the champagne glass had been cast off in favour of the vest and the beer can. The picture business was changing and the old stars, like the old-style movies, were fading. In December 1952, Cary Grant and Betsy Drake accepted the inevitable and set off for a long cruise to the Orient. Twenty years after he had first arrived in Hollywood behind the wheel of his Packard convertible, Cary Grant quietly disappeared, leaving what he called 'the hypocrisies of Hollywood' behind him.

CHAPTER SIX • LONELY HEART

In private, Cary Grant was never the relaxed, debonair man that he had so successfully created on the screen. Prone to profound self-doubt, and constantly frightened of failure, he could be both moody and irritable, but he would also take care to conceal those qualities in public — they were not the qualities a star was expected to demonstrate. Only his friends knew what he was really like. But now one old friend, Moss Hart, who had known him since his days on Broadway, had put part of his character into a screenplay.

Moss Hart's Norman Maine was a star, a complex, introspective leading man given to fits of depression who is drinking heavily when he meets a young actress anxious to make her reputation. They fall in love and marry, but his career begins inexorably to wane as hers takes off. Finally, at the climax of Hart's screenplay, the ageing male star walks out into the Pacific and drowns himself.

The story was not entirely new. The columnist Adela Rogers St John had written an earlier version, which George Cukor had directed for RKO as *What Price Hollywood?* in 1932, and five years later Dorothy Parker had worked on another version, this time for the director William Wellman, when it was retitled *A Star Is Born*. But Hart had deepened his portrait of the ageing star for his screenplay, which George Cukor was going to make for Warners. Judy Garland was to play the young actress, and Hart, Cukor and Garland all knew exactly whom they wanted to play opposite her: Cary Grant. In the late summer of 1952, before Grant disappeared from Hollywood, Cukor had invited Cary Grant to his house and asked him to read a section of Hart's script. Cukor tried everything he could to persuade Grant to play Norman Maine. Then Hart and Garland tried to persuade him. But Grant flatly refused. He was leaving for a trip around the world with Betsy, and he did not want even to think about movies. The more Cukor tried, the more stubborn Grant became. He would not do it. Both men knew the unspoken reason for his refusal. Norman Maine was too close to Cary Grant. He could not bear to reveal his own fears to the cinema audience.

On the steamer to Japan, Grant told his wife, 'I feel free for the first time in

'If I give the impression of being a man without a care in the world it is because people with problems always try to give that impression. We are all the opposite of what we appear to be.'

Left: A reflective Grant on a visit to London after his 'retirement' from the movies in 1953.
Above right: Sophia Loren was one of the women who rekindled his interest.

my life', and in the weeks to come they set about isolating themselves from the world they had known before. They invented their own private language. 'You look thoughtative,' he would tell her, before describing himself as 'happily tearful'. They experimented with hypnotism. She wanted to use it to help him to give up smoking sixty cigarettes a day. 'She put me in a trance,' he remembered

EVEN AT FIFTY, GRANT
MANAGED TO LOOK YOUNGER
THAN EVER ON THE SET.

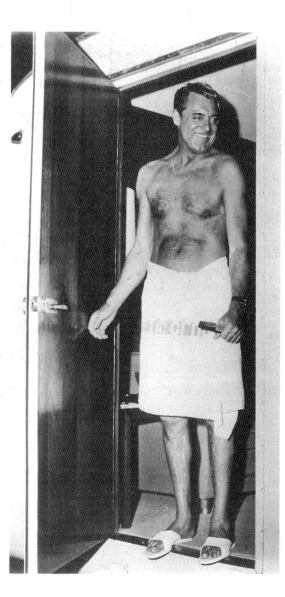

later, 'and planted a post-hypnotic suggestion that I would stop smoking. We went to sleep and the next morning when I reached for a cigarette, just as I always did, I took one puff and instantly felt nauseated.' They tried self-hypnotism, to help themselves sleep. They experimented with health-food diets and yoga as ways of calming down. But this did not entirely obliterate the morose moods that would sometimes flood over Grant when he and Betsy were alone together. Nevertheless, the trip helped. Visiting US servicemen in army hospitals, seeing Japan and then Hong Kong, seemed to provide him with a fresh perspective.

Back in his house in Palm Springs in the late spring of 1953, Grant started reading Plato's dialogues and the Greek plays, as well as biographies of Albert Schweitzer and Sigmund Freud. He and Betsy even consulted Ernest Holmes, the founder of the Church of Religious Science. As he was to admit later, 'I was a self-centred bore until the age of forty. I didn't have time for reading. Now I'm reading, absorbing, listening and learning about the world and myself.' In 1953 Grant's search for himself — a search which was to continue throughout the 1950s and into the 1960s — was relentless. Yet he remained troubled, never quite at peace with himself. His preoccupation with money persisted, as did his craving

for affection. He still longed for his mother to acknowledge how much he had accomplished. In the end only the movies could provide the recognition he craved, and as 1954 wore on Betsy Drake came to realize it.

At the end of 1954, Cary Grant was still only fifty and looked a decade younger. He was a star, and Betsy slowly came to understand that, in spite of what he told her, he was not ready to disappear into obscurity. Part of him wanted to be alone, certainly, but another part missed the rapture that only an audience could bring. There was something in the audience's acclaim that stilled his insecurity, proving that he deserved to be loved.

No one understood Cary Grant's ambivalence better than Alfred Hitchcock. He knew the demons that pursued Grant, and he also knew that he liked to be tempted, particularly by the right script and the right leading lady. Hitchcock had recently completed two films with Hollywood's latest female star, Grace Kelly — *Dial M for Murder* and *Rear Window*, and she had just won her first Academy Award for *The Country Girl*. In an astonishing rise to prominence, she had made only six films in a screen career stretching back a mere three years. But Hitchcock had recognized the passion that lay beneath Kelly's beautiful, glacial exterior, just as he had seen the menace beneath Grant's smile. Now the irony of making one of the screen's legendary charmers into the object of Grace Kelly's desire fascinated him, and he suspected that it would be a temptation that Cary Grant would not be able to refuse.

When Hitchcock had first sent Grant the script for *To Catch a Thief*, he had received the customary refusal. But the director was not put off. He just kept on explaining his plans. The film was to be shot in the South of France, the hero was a retired cat burglar caught up in a string of robberies which he did not commit, and he was to become involved with a young woman who believed he was a thief but who fell in love with him nevertheless. Finally, Hitchcock told Grant that his co-star was to be Grace Kelly. As Grant admitted later, 'I didn't want to do the film. It was only when Hitch told me

HITCHCOCK FINALLY TEMPTED GRANT BACK TO WORK IN 1955. THE DIRECTOR'S OFFER OF HOLLYWOOD'S NEW PRINCESS, GRACE KELLY, AS HIS CO-STAR IN *TO CATCH A THIEF* PROVED IRRESISTIBLE.

The Royal Performance Film

PARAMOUNT Presents

CARY GRANT *AND* GRACE KELLY

IN

ALFRED HITCHCOCK'S

TO CATCH A THIEF

COLOUR BY TECHNICOLOR

VISTAVISION
MOTION PICTURE HIGH FIDELITY

with JESSIE ROYCE LANDIS · JOHN WILLIAMS

Directed by ALFRED HITCHCOCK · Screenplay by JOHN MICHAEL HAYES · Based on the novel by DAVID DODGE

TWO YEARS AWAY HAD
MATURED GRANT'S CHARM.
NOW HE WAS EVEN MORE
ATTRACTIVE AND MORE
RELAXED ON THE SCREEN, A
QUALITY HITCHCOCK SUBTLY
EXPLOITED IN THEIR THIRD
FILM TOGETHER (ABOVE).

I'd play opposite Grace Kelly that I did accept.'

So, in November 1954, two years after he had left the set of *Dream Wife* and set off for the Far East, Grant left Palm Springs for the French Riviera. There had been some agonizing discussions with Betsy, but Hitchcock's bait

had proved too tempting. Besides, Paramount had guaranteed that he would never have to film after six in the evening and that he would be staying in the most luxurious surroundings, the Hotel du Cap in Antibes. They had also guaranteed him a percentage of the film's takings.

As filming got under way, Grant became steadily more impressed with his twenty-six-year-old co-star's ability, both as an actress and as a comedienne. Kelly concentrated as much as he did while they were shooting, and she could not only ad-lib as quickly as he could, she

was also never afraid to do so. 'She really listens, she's right there with you,' Grant would say admiringly to Hitchcock. Kelly seemed to embody everything that he most admired in a woman — style, elegance, grace and a certain mystery. 'She was the most beautiful woman I'd ever known and she had the most incredible ESP about me,' he would admit later. 'She could almost read my thoughts.' Grace Kelly was to become Cary Grant's favourite leading lady. 'She was the most memorable and honest actress I've ever worked with.... Grace had a kind of serenity, a calmness,

Left: With Grace Kelly rehearsing a scene in *To Catch a Thief*.
Right: 'Here, hold them... they're the most beautiful thing in the world.' Grace Kelly was referring to her diamonds. Not every movie-goer believed her.

that I hadn't arrived at at that point in my life. She was so relaxed in front of the camera that she made it look easy. She was astonishing.'

The screen relationship between Cary Grant and Grace Kelly in *To Catch a Thief* became the most openly sexual of any of his films. And, like Bergman in *Notorious*, Hitchcock made her the aggressor. When Kelly first kisses Grant in the corridor of their hotel, Hitchcock said later, 'It's as though she'd unzipped Cary's fly.' Shortly afterwards, Hitchcock had her look up at him, wearing a magnificent necklace and a distinctly low-cut gown, and murmur, 'Here, hold them...they're the most beautiful thing in the world, and the one thing you can't resist.' She was referring, of course, to the jewels. But Kelly's own sense of humour also came out in the picnic scene, when she ad-libbed part of her dialogue. Offering him a piece of chicken she asked, 'Do you want a leg or a breast?' 'You make the choice,' he replied, and she went on, 'Tell me, how long has it been?' 'Since what?' There was a delicate pause. 'Since you were last in America.'

But when the film opened in New York, in late August 1955, it looked as though Grant might have been mistaken to come out of 'retirement'. The critics dismissed it. *Variety* particularly disliked John Michael Hayes's screenplay, based on David Dodge's novel: 'Billed as a comedy-mystery, it stacks up as a drawn-out pretentious piece that seldom hits comedy level. As a mystery it fails to mystify, though it does confuse.' The magazine concluded, 'This film won't enhance the prestige of either the stars or the producer-director.' Meanwhile Bosley Crowther in *The New York Times* suggested it 'does nothing but give out a good exciting time'. That, however, was exactly what the audience wanted. *To Catch a Thief* became one of Paramount's biggest box-office successes in 1955.

Mike Todd wanted to exploit Cary Grant's return to the screen without a moment's delay. Ebullient, imaginative and a born showman, Todd was planning to assemble the largest collection of stars ever seen in a single film. The story he planned to use was Jules Verne's *Around the World in Eighty Days*, and the single star among the forty-four with whom he wanted his audience to identify was Cary Grant, as the indomitable hero, Phileas Fogg.

Grant was flattered, but far from certain. The more Todd described the project, with its exotic locations all over the world, the more it seemed to him to be a travelogue rather than a film. There did not seem much room for him to create a character, even though the script was being written specifically for him by S.J. Perelman, John Farrow and James Poe. Grant was not 'sure that he could make it work'. Even Todd's offer that he could own half the film himself, together with half its profits, did not convince him. Eventually Grant turned it down, and Todd offered the role instead to his

YOU HAVE NEVER SEEN ITS LIKE —AND MAY NEVER SEE ITS EQUAL!

CARY GRANT
as the pride

FRANK SINATRA
as the passion

SOPHIA LOREN
as the woman who set them both on fire!

IN Stanley Kramer's MONUMENTAL FILMING OF

"THE PRIDE and THE PASSION"

IN 1957 GRANT WORKED
WITH THE WOMAN WHO
WOULD BECOME A GREAT
PASSION, SOPHIA LOREN.

old friend David Niven. *Around the World in Eighty Days* went on to become one of the highest-grossing films in Hollywood history.

It was not the only successful film that Grant was to turn down in 1955. Another producer, Sam Spiegel, was getting together a picture for Columbia based on the story of the British prisoners of war forced by the Japanese to work on the notorious Burma Railway. The English director David Lean, who was working on the script with Carl Foreman, had already cast Alec Guinness as the English officer obsessed with building *The Bridge on the River*

Kwai, but he and Spiegel both wanted Grant to play the American sent to destroy the bridge. Once again, Grant was not sure. He did not know whether he wanted to spend quite so long on location in Ceylon. He was not being offered the leading role. The jungle sounded as though it might be taxing. Irritated by his dithering, Columbia sent the script to William Holden, who accepted without hesitation. As Grant recalled later, 'By then, of course, I realized what a great part I'd lost.'

Betsy Drake had given up her own career when her husband 'retired' at the end of 1952, and his return to work on *To Catch a Thief* had not been exactly what she had planned. In fact, she had been prepared to allow him to go back to filming only on the understanding that there would still be time for them to spend long periods away from Hollywood. But even that had become a fantasy. Their quiet evenings in Palm Springs were a thing of the past. By the time Grace Kelly married Prince Rainier of Monaco in April 1956, it had become abundantly clear to the third Mrs Cary Grant that there was little point in her sitting at home waiting for her husband. Grant could not even go to the wedding — he had already started work on a new film.

Stanley Kramer, the producer of *High Noon*, wanted to win Grant an Oscar, just as he had done for Gary Cooper, and he had decided to use a C.S.

Forester story about the Napoleonic Wars, *The Gun*, to do so. Four years earlier, Spiegel and John Houston had won Bogart an Oscar with a Forester story, *The African Queen*, and Kramer thought that lightning might strike twice. With a screenplay by Edward and Edna Anhalt, the film was to be called *The Pride and the Passion*, and Kramer was convinced that the historical drama would be a good opportunity for Grant to break away from his familiar style. His principal co-star was to be Frank Sinatra, as the leader of the Spanish guerrilla forces, and Kramer had decided to cast the almost unknown Italian actress Sophia Loren as the leading lady. It was to be her first film in English.

Kramer had also decided to shoot the film entirely on location in Spain. It

was a mistake, making it almost impossibly arduous. The heat of the Spanish summer, and the need for thousands of extras as a backdrop to the huge cannon that played a central role in the story, slowed filming down persistently, and proved too much for Frank Sinatra. With five weeks of shooting still to go, he walked off the set and left for the United States. Cary Grant and Sophia Loren were left to carry on alone. By that time they had become close friends.

At first Grant had been determined not to reveal too much of himself to

AFTER THEY HAD MET FOR THE FIRST TIME ON THE SET OF *THE PRIDE AND THE PASSION*, SOPHIA LOREN ADMITTED, 'I WAS FASCINATED.' IT WAS A FASCINATION THAT ALMOST LED TO MARRIAGE.

Loren. But as the weeks had passed, he had confided in her more and more. 'It disturbed him that although he had been married three times, he had never really sustained a relationship with a woman,' she explained later. He had talked about his self-doubts and his early life. 'I was fascinated with him, with his warmth, affection, intelligence and his wonderfully dry, mischievous sense of humour,' she remembered. He showered her with flowers, and they fell in love.

That did not make the shooting of *The Pride and the Passion* any easier. Grant was suddenly intent on trying to persuade Loren to marry him, telling her

NO MATTER HOW HARD HE TRIED, GRANT COULD NOT QUITE PERSUADE SOPHIA LOREN TO MARRY HIM. 'I WISH I WEREN'T SO MIXED UP,' SHE TOLD HIM AS THEY PARTED ON THE LAST DAY OF FILMING.

woman he could 'commit himself to'. 'I never doubted for a second that Cary loved me as much as I could hope to be loved by a man,' Loren was to explain later. On the last night of filming, she told him, 'I wish I weren't so mixed up and confused. One day I am pulled one way and the next day another. I don't know what's going to happen.' Grant said simply, 'Why don't we just get married and discuss all this afterwards?' A trembling Sophia Loren left the next morning, on her way to Greece to appear with Alan Ladd in *Boy on a Dolphin*. Her co-star meanwhile began the long trip back to Hollywood, hopeful that she would finally agree to become the fourth Mrs Cary Grant.

The passions that raged during the shooting of *The Pride and the Passion* were not reflected on the screen. Sinatra's abrupt departure had hurt the picture, and not even the most determined efforts by Grant and Loren could save it. 'The whir of the cameras often seems as loud as the thunderous cannonades,' commented *Time*, when it opened in July 1957. 'It evidently takes more than dedication, co-operative multitudes and four million dollars to shoot history in the face.' In spite of the unfavourable reviews, the film turned out to be a box-office success. And it put Cary Grant back on the list of Hollywood's top ten male stars.

that he was ready 'to renounce everything', even though both his wife and Loren's married lover, Carlo Ponti, were due at the location at any moment. When Betsy arrived it did not take her long to realize that her husband's attitude towards her had changed. Deeply hurt, she set off back to California, to start work on a film for Fox called *Will Success Spoil Rock Hunter?* Her journey took her across the Atlantic on board the Italian liner *Andrea Doria*. On the night of 25 July 1956, in patchy fog off the Newfoundland coast, the ship was

rammed by the Swedish liner *Stockholm*, and nearly 1,200 passengers and crew were forced to abandon ship within half an hour. Forty-three people lost their lives. Betsy Drake was not one of them, but, as she put it afterwards, 'I don't think I have ever loved Cary quite as much as I did the night I thought I would never live to see him again.'

Grant did not immediately abandon *The Pride and the Passion* to be with his wife. Instead he remained on location, apparently more convinced than ever that in Sophia Loren he had found a

On the surface, life seemed to go on as before in the Grants' homes in Beverly Hills and Palm Springs, but underneath everything had changed. Betsy Drake was working again, opposite Jayne Mansfield and Tony Randall at Fox, and Grant was sending flowers to Sophia Loren. Their attempt to remove themselves from Hollywood had failed, and both now sensed that their marriage had failed with it. For the moment, however, neither wanted to be the first to acknowledge it. That would have been too painful.

A failing marriage did not prevent Grant playing the romantic lead on the screen, however. In February 1957, he went back to Fox to do precisely that, and to work with Leo McCarey for the third time. The director's health had been poor, but the studio wanted him to make another romantic comedy with Cary Grant and, after some thought, McCarey had decided to remake his own 1939 hit, *Love Affair*, which had originally starred Charles Boyer and Irene Dunne. The story of a couple who fall in love while crossing the Atlantic, then agree to part for six months while the man tries to establish a new career as a commercial artist, McCarey called it his 'favourite love story'. When the woman fails to keep their rendezvous after six months, the man assumes she has changed her mind, although, in fact, she has been hurt in an accident. In *An Affair to Remember*, as McCarey's new version was to be called, Grant was to appear opposite Deborah Kerr, his co-star on the disastrous *Dream Wife*.

When shooting started, McCarey noticed a significant change in the 'tortured worrier' he remembered from *The Awful Truth*. Grant seemed far more assured and relaxed than he had done in the past, and that communicated itself in

SADDENED, GRANT TOOK REFUGE WITH HIS FRIENDS DEBORAH KERR AND DIRECTOR LEO MCCAREY IN 1957 TO MAKE *AN AFFAIR TO REMEMBER*.

TIME CALLED IT 'A
SACCHARINE TRIFLE', BUT
AN AFFAIR TO REMEMBER
REMAINS ONE OF
HOLLYWOOD'S BEST-LOVED
ROMANCES, AS *SLEEPLESS
IN SEATTLE* WAS TO BE
THIRTY-SIX YEARS LATER.

ad-lib for a cabin boy: 'I've heard so much about you.' When Grant asked what the boy had heard, McCarey gave him the response, 'I don't know. Whenever they start to talk about you they make me leave the room.' It was McCarey's way of telling the audience 'the opinion people had about Grant without having to underline it'.

When *An Affair to Remember* was released in July 1957, a week before *The Pride and the Passion*, some critics carped at its old-fashioned quality. The *New Yorker* dismissed it as 'awfully maudlin', while *Time* commented, 'Only sensitive acting from Deborah Kerr and Cary Grant saves this saccharine trifle from suffocating in its sentimental wrappings.' By contrast the *Los Angeles Times* was full of praise, both for the picture itself and for McCarey: 'To bring back to the screen within twenty years an enormously appealing picture subject, and cause it to appear as effective, if not even better than the original, is a true achievement in film-making.' The paper complimented McCarey for doing so 'movingly and impressively'. It was this second version of the story that was to inspire a fresh passion for romantic comedy in 1993 in Nora Ephron's *Sleepless in Seattle*, with Tom Hanks and Meg Ryan.

By the time *An Affair to Remember*

his performance. 'The difference between *Love Affair* and *An Affair to Remember*,' McCarey explained, 'is very simply the difference between Charles Boyer and Cary Grant. Grant could never really mask his sense of humour —which is extraordinary — and that's why the second version is funnier.' But the director also marked his star's old habits by inserting a carefully planned

was released, Grant was shooting again. He had started work in May on *Kiss Them for Me*, another comedy for Fox, this time directed by the thirty-three-year-old Stanley Donen. Donen had started his career as a dancer and choreographer, going on to co-direct a string of MGM musicals, including *On the Town* and *Singin' in the Rain*. Written by Jules Epstein and based on Frederick Wakeman's novel *Shore Leave*, his new film was an inconsequential romp depicting the adventures of three navy pilots on shore leave in San Francisco. Fox's latest contract star, Jayne Mansfield, and Suzy Parker, a twenty-year-old model newly turned actress, were Grant's co-stars, and the whole shoot was designed to take just ten weeks. As soon as it was over, Grant

and Betsy were planning to take another trip to England to see his mother. Things did not go according to plan, however. While Grant was filming Sophia Loren arrived in Hollywood. Now when the cast of *Kiss Them for Me* went to see their rushes each evening at 6.30, Sophia Loren suddenly took to appearing and Cary Grant proceeded 'to fall in love with her all over again'. It did not make life any easier for Stanley Donen. But no matter what emotional crises Grant was facing, the young director did everything he could to make the filming easy. Sadly, his efforts did little to help his film. When it was released in November 1957, Bosley Crowther remarked in *The New York Times* that Grant 'seems somewhat over-age for this kind of assignment'.

LEFT: In *Kiss Them for Me*, with Suzy Parker, Grant once again found himself pursued by Hollywood's latest sex symbol, Jayne Mansfield – even though he was now fifty-three.

Over-age or not, at fifty-three Cary Grant was most certainly in love, and, just as he had with Betsy Drake, he was determined to appear on the screen with Sophia Loren. Suddenly, a chance presented itself. Jack Rose and Mel Shavelson, who had written *Room for One More* for him and Betsy, had worked up another story about children, called *Houseboat*. This time, instead of being orphans, the children had lost their mother and were trying to remake a relationship with their father. When

LEFT: Sophia Loren came to Hollywood in 1958 to make *Houseboat,* and re-ignited Grant's passion. The movie's climax was their wedding (*RIGHT*), but off the set Loren married Carlo Ponti. The *Hollywood Reporter* still called Grant's performance 'just about flawless'.

the project had first been discussed Betsy had been keen, not least because she was eager to appear with her husband again. Now Paramount wanted to make the film, with Shavelson as director and Rose as producer — but they did not want it to star Betsy Drake, especially as they had just signed Sophia Loren to a four-picture deal.

Paramount pointed out that *The Pride and the Passion* had demonstrated just how successful a combination Cary Grant and Sophia Loren could be at the box-office, and, after lengthy heart-searching, Grant reluctantly accepted their suggestion. A desolate Betsy Drake left Hollywood with her husband for their long-planned trip to see his mother, but when Grant returned to Los Angeles to start work on *Houseboat,* he was alone.

Filming did not prove easy. Grant was edgy. He was in love with Loren but frightened that she would never abandon Carlo Ponti, and only too aware that his third marriage was probably over whatever happened. Once again his screen life seemed mysteriously to echo his own. The climax of *Houseboat* was to be the wedding of Cary Grant and Sophia Loren, but suddenly, with only two days to go before the filming of the wedding itself, Louella Parsons reported that Loren and Carlo Ponti had been married 'by proxy' by two lawyers in Juarez, Mexico. Loren said later that her screen 'marriage' to Grant 'was painful for me, too, his make-believe bride. I could not help thinking of all those lovely times in Spain.' But when the film's minister pronounced them man and wife, Grant simply said to her, 'I hope you will be very happy' and kissed her on both cheeks. The moment shooting was completed he walked off the set, and within a few days he had disappeared

from Hollywood altogether, to find Betsy in England.

With Loren and Ponti now firmly settled in Beverly Hills, Cary Grant could not bring himself to return to California, and was only too happy to accept Stanley Donen's suggestion of a new project which could be shot in England. Donen thought Grant had been wonderful opposite Ingrid Bergman in *Notorious*, and he wanted to put them together again. He also thought he could persuade his friend Norman Krasna to allow him to move the location of his 1953 Broadway play, *Kind Sir*, from New York to London, as the basis of his

new Grant and Bergman movie. If he could do so, Warners had agreed to finance the production and guarantee Grant's customary fee of $300,000.

Grant still admired Bergman as much as he had done when they finished *Notorious*. But his view was no longer shared by majority of the American cinema-going public. Bergman had not made a film in Hollywood since 1949, when her virtuous screen image had been shattered by the revelation that she had left her husband and their daughter Pia for the Italian director Roberto Rossellini, and that she was pregnant with Rossellini's child. Though Bergman

had subsequently married Rossellini, and had a son and twin daughters with him, 'Suddenly the American public that elevated her to the point of idolatry cast her down, vilified her, and boycotted her films', in the words of *The New York Times*. But Grant had remained a friend. Indeed, in March 1957, he had proved how much he cared for Bergman. He

AFTER SOPHIA LOREN'S MARRIAGE, GRANT FLED HOLLYWOOD FOR LONDON TO MAKE *INDISCREET* FOR DIRECTOR STANLEY DONEN, WITH HIS OLD FRIEND AND CO-STAR FROM *NOTORIOUS*, INGRID BERGMAN.

THE AFFECTION INGRID BERGMAN AND GRANT FELT FOR EACH OTHER WAS ABUNDANTLY CLEAR ON THE SCREEN. *INDISCREET* BECAME ONE OF GRANT'S FAVOURITE FILMS, AND ONE OF THE BIGGEST HITS OF 1958.

had broken one of his own strict rules and agreed to appear on television to accept an Academy Award on her behalf for her performance in *Anastasia*. Conquering his own stage fright, he had told the television audience, 'Dear Ingrid, if you can hear me now or will see this televised film later, I want you to know that each of the other nominees and all the people with whom you worked on *Anastasia*, and Hitch, and Leo McCarey, and indeed everyone here tonight, send you congratulations and love and admiration and every affectionate thought.'

So when Stanley Donen arrived in Rome a few months later to discuss the possibility of her making a film with Grant, Ingrid Bergman had told him firmly, 'I'm going to do the picture. Just tell me what it is.' By the time she got to London to start filming, however, she was back in the headlines. Her relationship with Rossellini had broken up. Once again Grant came to her rescue. At a press conference, he told the assembled reporters when they badgered her about her private life, 'You can't ask a lady

that. Ask me the same question and I'll give you an answer. So you're not interested in my life? It's twice as colourful as Ingrid's.' What the reporters did not realize was that Grant's marriage, too, was once more on the brink of collapse.

Grant and Donen's new film, for which they had formed a new company, Grandon Productions, was another light comedy. Norman Krasna had indeed adapted his Broadway play for the screen, and retitled it *Indiscreet*. Bergman played a famous actress and Grant a dashing American diplomat protecting his bachelor status by pretending to be married. Grant himself had suggested one of Bergman's best lines of dialogue: 'How dare you make love to me and not be a married man?' He felt sure it would make every other line in the picture funnier. *Indiscreet* was to become one of his favourite films, and one of Warner Brothers' biggest box-office hits when it was released in May 1958. 'The actors volley Krasna's ebullient dialogue with masterful adroitness and manage romance with a subtlety that detracts

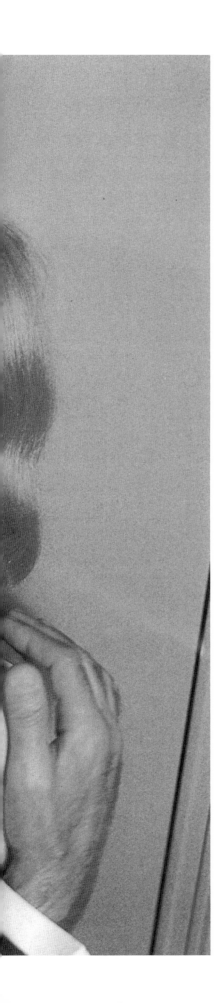

Left: Eva Marie Saint was not Grace Kelly, but she was every bit as graceful a foil in North by Northwest in 1959. He was one of Hollywood's biggest box-office stars.

not for a moment from its ardour,' as *Newsweek* put it.

Meanwhile Cary Grant was struggling to see whether he could save his marriage. It was no easy task. After the shooting of *Indiscreet* was completed in December 1957, he had taken Betsy to Monte Carlo to stay on Aristotle Onassis's yacht and visit Prince Rainier and Princess Grace, but gloomy memories of the past had gradually overwhelmed them. So, in the New Year, he left Betsy in Europe and took a trip to Moscow with Sam Spiegel, Howard Hawks's former wife Slim and the author Truman Capote. Then he set off back to California.

Alfred Hitchcock and he were planning their fourth film together. Ernest Lehman, who had just collaborated with Clifford Odets on the script of *Sweet Smell of Success*, had been working on Hitchcock's idea of a movie about a chase across the United States which would culminate on the massive stone monument to four presidents at Mount Rushmore, South Dakota. One of Hitch's original titles had been 'The Man in Lincoln's Nose', but he had amended it to 'In a Northerly Direction' before changing it again to *North by Northwest*.

Hitchcock wanted to make his new film the ultimate exploration of the character that he and Cary Grant had perfected: the man to whom terrible things happen but who nevertheless

never seems to lose control. It was to be an American version of Hitch's English thriller *The Thirty-Nine Steps*, with Grant every bit as wrongly accused as Richard Hannay and just as determined to clear his name. For the woman who was to share the journey with him, Grant had suggested Sophia Loren, but she had turned the part down, deciding instead to return to Italy.

In Loren's place Hitchcock had suggested Eva Marie Saint. Cool, blonde and attractive, she was closer to Grace Kelly than to Loren, but her calm exterior seemed to hint at Kelly's passion and the director admired her performance in *On the Waterfront*, which had won her an Oscar. Nevertheless, Grant was irritated and

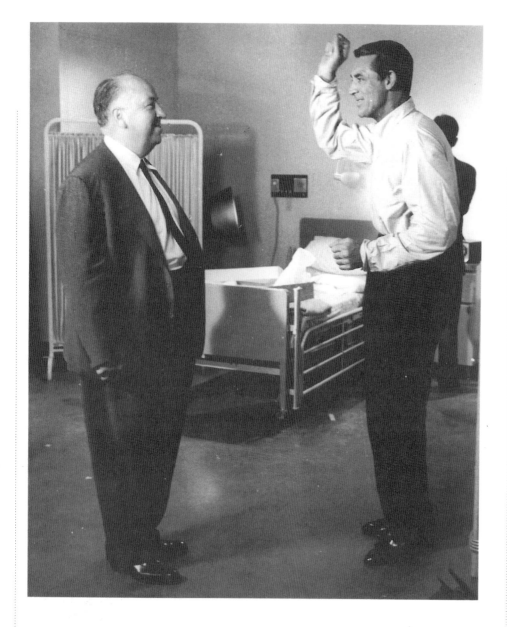

IN *NORTH BY NORTHWEST*
ALFRED HITCHCOCK CREATED
THE ULTIMATE VERSION OF HIS
STAR'S SCREEN PERSONA:
THE MAN TERRIFYING THINGS
HAPPEN TO. NEVER MORE SO
THAN IN THE CROP-DUSTER
CHASE.

unsettled when he started work with her in the early summer of 1958. No sooner had he begun than he decided the film would be a disaster, and tried, as he had done so many times before, to get out of making it altogether. Hitchcock and MGM, who were financing the picture, stood firm. Grant had signed a contract. Whatever he felt about the script, or the cast, or anything else for that matter, he still had to finish it. A reluctant Grant accepted defeat.

One reason for his nervousness was that his image as one of the cinema's great lovers was about to be put in jeopardy. On 17 October 1958, while *North by Northwest* was still shooting, he and Betsy Drake announced that they had decided to live apart. 'We have had, and always shall have, a deep love and respect for each other,' their joint statement read, 'but, alas, our marriage has not brought us the happiness we fully expected and mutually desired. So, since we have no children needful of our

affection, it is consequently best that we separate for a while' They concluded by insisting that there were no plans for divorce, but Alfred Hitchcock, like most of Grant's friends, knew that was inevitable. It provoked him to insert a line of dialogue into the picture they were finishing together: he had Grant tell Eva Marie Saint, 'My wives divorced me. I think they said I led too dull a life.'

Grant's attractiveness on the screen, however, had never been greater. When *Houseboat* opened in November 1958, the *Hollywood Reporter* described his performance as 'just about flawless', adding, 'With sure artistry, he seems unconscious of the farcical nature of the ridiculous events that overwhelm him.' It was a skill that had made him one of the highest paid actors in the industry, earning an average of $500,000 a picture after his 10 per cent gross profit participations were included. Only Marlon Brando and Frank Sinatra could guarantee to make as much money as he did from films, and films were not his only source of income. He was also still investing carefully in stocks and shares, real estate and currency.

After the separation, Grant provided Betsy Drake with financial support and a house in the hills above Sunset Boulevard. She had become his closest friend, a confidante whom he felt he could always trust, rather than a lover. There had been none of the tempestuous quarrels between them that had coloured his relationships with Virginia Cherrill and Barbara Hutton. Betsy may have looked at him a little sadly as their marriage gradually ebbed away, but she never became his enemy. And it was

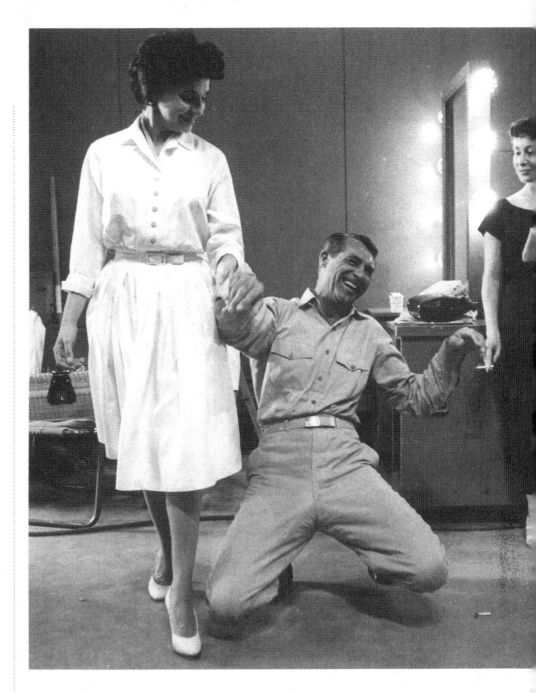

GRANT HAD NOT BEEN
ON A SUBMARINE SINCE
DESTINATION TOKYO
FIFTEEN YEARS BEFORE, BUT
UNIVERSAL TEMPTED HIM BACK
ON BOARD WITH *OPERATION
PETTICOAT*, DIRECTED BY
BLAKE EDWARDS.

Betsy who now introduced Grant to the psychotherapist who was to transform his life still further. Late in 1958, she started sessions with Dr Mortimer Hartman and soon afterwards recommended him to her husband. Grant was to become Hartman's most famous and most controversial patient, the first Hollywood star to admit to using the hallucinogenic drug LSD.

After Grant had taken LSD, Hartman asked him to lie on a couch in a darkened room, with his eyes masked and plugs in his ears, to 'relive their past'. Each session could last up to six hours, and Hartman was convinced that the drug helped to 'facilitate the progress of psychotherapy'. Grant would usually be delivered to his Beverly Hills clinic by a chauffeur on Saturday mornings, to be collected again in the late afternoon.' I had become dissatisfied with me,' he admitted later. 'I took LSD in the hope it would make me feel better about myself.'

Cary Grant was to use LSD more than one hundred times before the drug was finally declared illegal by the United States government in 1965, and he was to insist that it never had any harmful effect upon him. 'You become free of the usual discipline. I became happier for it, and the insights I gained dispelled many of the fears I had prior to that time.' In the sessions, he talked through the

despair of his childhood, and his relationships with his parents and his wives. 'I found it extremely valuable. It did me a great deal of good. It brought up all those guilts, all the nightmares I'd been holding down.'

Indeed, Grant became so enthusiastic about the value of LSD and the benefits that it brought him that he extolled its virtues during the shooting of his next picture. Universal had approached him to make *Operation Petticoat*,

written by Stanley Shapiro and Maurice Richlin, a romantic comedy about the exploits of a group of nurses on board a pink-painted submarine in the first weeks of the Second World War. The director was to be the thirty-seven-year-old former screenwriter Blake Edwards, and Grant's co-star was to be Tony Curtis, who had just played a saxophone player forced to pretend he is a woman in Billy Wilder's *Some Like It Hot*, giving in the process a perfect

RIGHT: GRANT'S CO-STAR
JOAN O'BRIEN SCRATCHES
HIS BACK ON THE SET OF
OPERATION PETTICOAT IN
1959. ALSO STARRING
TONY CURTIS, IT BECAME
ONE OF UNIVERSAL'S
BIGGEST HITS EVER.

April, the American newspapers were filled with reports that Cary Grant had been taking hallucinogenic drugs.

But these revelations did nothing to harm his appeal. When *North by Northwest* opened in July, *Newsweek* confirmed that he and Hitchcock were 'two of the slickest operators before and behind the Hollywood cameras. Together they can be unbeatable.' *Variety* added, 'The mixture as before, suspense, intrigue, comedy, humour; but seldom has the concoction been served up so delectably or in so glossy a package.' The film was to become one of MGM's biggest box-office hits in 1959, taking more than $6 million in the United States alone.

Universal rushed out *Operation Petticoat* in December 1959 to capitalize on Grant's popularity, and were rewarded with more than $9.5 million in receipts at the American box-office. The film became the biggest hit in the studio's history, and made Grant over $3 million from his profit participation alone. Even the flimsy plot did not, for once, alienate the critics. *Variety* paid particular tribute to his performance: 'Grant is a living lesson in getting laughs without lines.... It is his reaction, blank, startled, etc., always underplayed, that creates or releases the humour.'

There seemed to be nothing Cary Grant touched that did not turn to gold.

imitation of Cary Grant. The studio agreed to give Grant a bungalow on their lot north of Hollywood, and to pay him $300,000 plus 25 per cent of the profits.

No sooner had the shooting of *Operation Petticoat* got under way in Key West, Florida, in the spring of 1959, than Cary Grant gave two highly untypical interviews. The man who had made his Hollywood reputation by never talking about himself suddenly revealed to the Hollywood columnist Joe Hyams, 'Each of us is dying for affection but we don't know how to go about getting it. Everything we do is affected by this longing. I wanted people to like me, but I went about it the wrong way.' He admitted that he had been undergoing psychotherapy and experimenting with LSD. By late

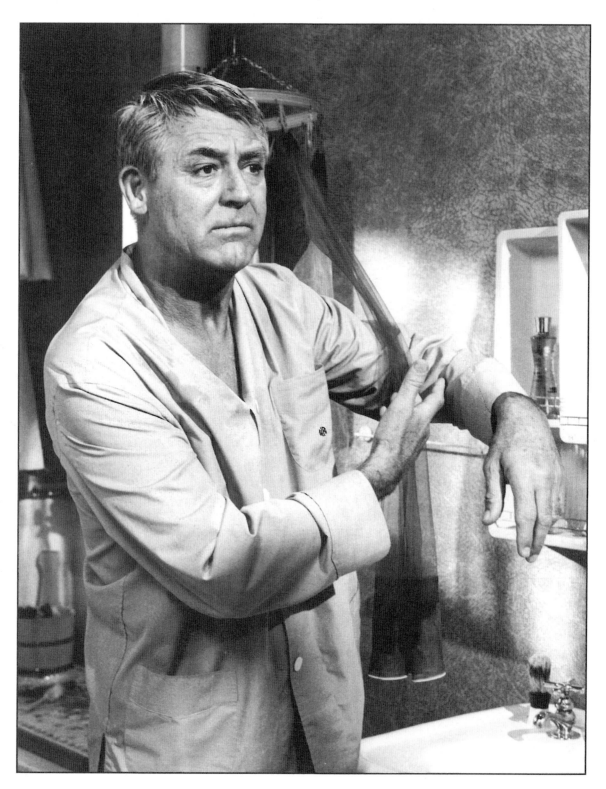

CHAPTER SEVEN • FINAL BOW

W

When Cary Grant went to visit his mother during the first days of January 1960, Elsie Leach was on the brink of her eighty-third birthday. Apart from her steel-grey hair, she showed hardly a sign of ageing. The small, fierce woman sat rigidly in front of her son, looking at him as she had always done, like an exhibit, a man whom she hardly knew.

One afternoon Grant took her out for a drive. 'Archie,' she said suddenly, 'you should dye your hair.' When he asked her why, she replied, 'Because it makes me look so old.'

Elsie Leach also told him to patch up his marriage with Betsy Drake. It was time for him 'to settle down', she said, and for a time it almost seemed as if he might. Grant and Betsy had gone to Bristol together to see his mother, and from there had returned to London to stay in a suite at the Savoy overlooking the Thames. With Elsie's words ringing in his ears, Grant took his wife for drives in the Rolls-Royce he had demanded from Warners for making *Indiscreet*. At other times Betsy would wander round

London while Grant talked to Stanley Donen about a new production they were planning to do together in London. Betsy did not particularly want to return to California, and Cary Grant was happy enough to work in England again.

Grant and Donen were hoping to repeat the success of *Indiscreet* by making another film version of a stage play, this time one by Hugh and Margaret Williams called *The Grass Is Greener*. A romantic comedy, it called for Grant to play the baffled Earl of Rhyall, whose wife, the Countess, falls in love with an American taking a tour of their stately home. He and Donen wanted Rex Harrison and Kay Kendall as the other two leading characters, with Deborah Kerr in support. But Kendall's sudden death, at the age of just thirty-three, had forced them to reconsider. Harrison withdrew, and eventually Donen suggested that Robert Mitchum should take his place, with Deborah Kerr playing the role intended for Kendall and Jean Simmons replacing Kerr as the fourth principal character.

Shooting began in April 1960 and progressed smoothly enough, although Robert Mitchum suggested afterwards that all he really needed was a girl at the side of the set to nudge him when Cary Grant came to the end of a speech, so that he could say 'Why? Really?'

'You can never go back. It's not possible. People are used to me as a certain kind of fellow, and I can't make that kind of film any more.'

AGEING IS NEVER EASY FOR A STAR, ESPECIALLY NOT FOR ONE WHO HAS BEEN PURSUED BY BEAUTIFUL WOMEN LIKE DORIS DAY (ABOVE RIGHT) FOR THREE DECADES. GRANT CHOSE *WALK DON'T RUN* IN 1966 (LEFT) TO BRING HIS CAREER TO AN END, RATHER THAN RISK TARNISHING HIS UNIQUE SCREEN IMAGE.

STILL WORKING, GRANT STARRED WITH DEBORAH KERR FOR THE THIRD TIME IN 1961 IN STANLEY DONEN'S *THE GRASS IS GREENER*.

Deborah Kerr remained a devoted admirer, however, paying tribute to Grant's professionalism, but insisting that he remained as he had always been — 'a very private person'. Grant, on the other hand, seemed a little distracted.

No matter what his mother may have hoped, in the wake of his fifty-sixth birthday in January, Cary Grant had become obsessed with having a young woman on his arm wherever he went, even though Betsy was in London with him. Soon after shooting started on *The Grass Is Greener*, he was seen with the singer Alma Cogan, provoking one columnist to speculate that they were in love. A week later Louella Parsons reported that Betsy Drake had suddenly left London after her husband had been seen 'holding hands' with Cogan. As the filming continued, he was also seen in the company of a number of other beautiful young actresses, including Haya Harareet, Ziva Rodann, Jackie Chan and Nancy Kovack.

One American newspaper called his a 'marriage on the instalment plan', but Grant took no notice. He was more concerned that the owners of the Radio City Music Hall in New York, who had planned to use *The Grass Is Greener* as their Christmas film in 1960, had suddenly changed their mind when they saw the first cut. They did not like it, and the Hollywood press were equally unimpressed. When it finally opened, *Variety* called it 'a generally tedious exercise', and the *Hollywood Reporter* added, 'The stars do not glitter, or even glow.... It is one of the year's most disappointing films.' *The New York Times* condemned Grant for looking 'mechanical and bored'.

In a sense he was, but there was little he could do about it. He had been a romantic leading man for thirty years, and had burnished his carefully created mask with a skill that few other stars could match. There was no soul-searching in his performances, no desperation to appear to be 'acting'. He had simply honed his talents until he

played himself to perfection on the screen. His style was almost self-plagiarism, but he could not summon up the courage to change it. It was the reason he had turned down an approach from Fox to play the alcoholic Scott Fitzgerald in *Beloved Infidel*, and another from Warners to play the cheery confidence trickster in *The Music Man*. Neither was a 'Cary Grant character'.

That was the reason Grant accepted an invitation from Universal and Robert Arthur, his producer on *Operation*

AN EYE FOR A PRETTY GIRL NEVER DESERTED HIM. IN 1961 GRANT MADE A POINT OF TALKING TO MARGO McKENDRY IN THE UNIVERSAL COMMISSARY WHEN SHE WAS BROUGHT OUT FOR A SCREEN TEST.

Petticoat, to make another romantic comedy. Universal wanted to use him opposite the studio's latest princess, Doris Day, whose hits included *Pillow Talk*, and had asked Stanley Shapiro to write a suitable script. They also offered Grant a minimum of $600,000 against 10 per cent of the gross receipts to appear in a part that was definitely a 'Cary Grant character'. The director was to be Delbert Mann, who had won an Oscar for his first feature, *Marty*, in 1956. Grant did not hesitate.

But neither Doris Day nor Delbert Mann ever felt that they knew the star they worked with on *That Touch of Mink*. 'Cary Grant was very conscious of ever detail,' Mann said later. 'And I'd never come across an actor like that before.... The challenge of acting seemed to have gone out of things for him. He was just playing Cary Grant.' Once again Grant was playing a millionaire, a bachelor uninterested in marriage until his Rolls-Royce splashes a small-town girl in the rain in New York. And then, in the best tradition of Cary Grant comedies, he has to persuade the girl that he is not such a wicked seducer after all, and that it is quite safe for her to marry him. It was a well-worn formula, and the critics wasted no time in pointing that out. 'Too often there's a hampering second-hand air about situation and joke,' *Variety* suggested, a gloss

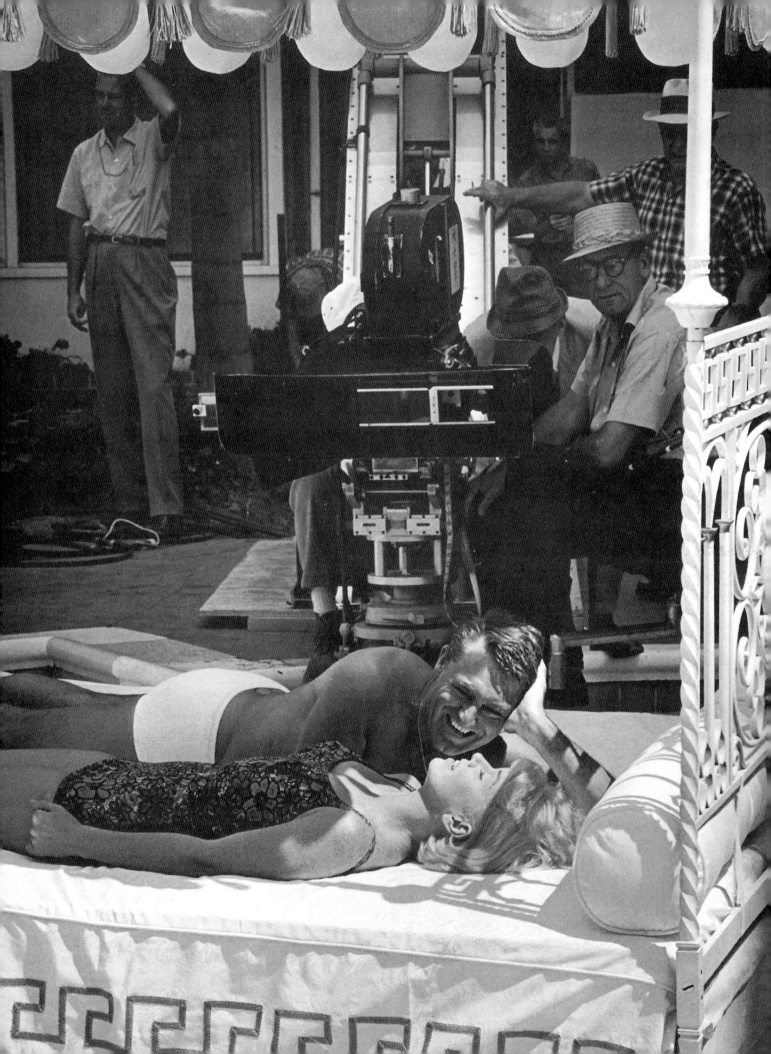

NOT EVERY WOMAN FELL AT
HIS FEET. DORIS DAY TOOK A
LITTLE TIME TO SUCCUMB IN
THAT TOUCH OF MINK (LEFT)
IN 1962, WHILE AUDREY
HEPBURN DIDN'T GIVE IN
TOO QUICKLY IN *CHARADE*
(RIGHT).

which did not obscure 'an essentially threadbare lining'. But that did nothing to lessen the film's success. When *That Touch of Mink* played at the Radio City Music Hall in the summer of 1962 it became the first film to take more than $1 million in a single cinema. It also earned Cary Grant more than $3 million from his profit participation.

He was now, unquestionably, one of the biggest box-office stars in the world, but his screen image had not brought him happiness. His use of LSD had come to an end, because Dr Hartman's experiments with the drug had been banned by the California Board of Medical Examiners. By the time *That Touch of Mink* was released his third marriage was over. Betsy Drake had decided that there was no point in trying to keep it alive any longer. Grant's latest relationship with a young actress, Greta Thyssen, had been the final straw, and Betsy had filed for divorce. At the hearing in August 1962, she claimed, just as Barbara Hutton had done before her, that Grant subjected her to mental cruelty. He 'left home for long periods', was 'apparently bored' with her, and 'preferred watching television to talking to me'. 'I was always in love with him and still am,' she told reporters. She then put Cary Grant and Hollywood firmly behind her, and turned instead to

studying psychotherapy and teaching drama. Grant wrote to his mother to explain that the divorce was inevitable and 'probably the best for both of us. At least I shall try to think so.' He signed the letter, 'Always, Archie.'

Cary Grant may not have cared for 'being married', as his newly divorced wife had told the Santa Monica Supreme Court, but he was utterly fascinated by courtship. There was a new object for his affections, a twenty-three-year-old actress called Dyan Cannon. Grant had first seen her on the television set in his bedroom when she made an appearance in a television series called *Malibu Run*. The next morning he went to considerable lengths to track her down, and he

courted her as relentlessly as he had once courted Betsy Drake.

No sooner had his third divorce been finalized than Grant left Hollywood again for Europe and another film with Stanley Donen. But on his way to Paris to meet the director he stopped in Philadelphia to catch the touring version of a Broadway comedy called *The Fun Couple*, in which Dyan Cannon was appearing. With tawny blonde hair and hazel eyes, Cannon was the daughter of a deacon in the Baptist Church and had arrived in Hollywood at the age of seventeen to find work as an actress. Instead she found herself working as a model and a beautician until a screen test had resulted in more than 200 parts

AUDREY HEPBURN BECAME
ONE OF HIS FAVOURITE
CO-STARS, EVEN THOUGH
THEY WORKED TOGETHER
JUST ONCE, ON CHARADE
FOR UNIVERSAL, RELEASED
IN 1963. SHE CALLED HIM
'A MYSTIC'.

on television. Suddenly, Cary Grant was fascinated by her.

No matter how much he may have pursued beautiful young women off the screen, however, he was utterly determined not to allow the screen image of Cary Grant to become a lecherous old man. Indeed he insisted that in *Charade*, the new film Donen was planning, he would not appear as a seducer. Instead, he wanted the young screenwriter, Peter Stone, to make sure that it was his female co-star who was the sexual aggressor. Stone, on his first feature, was only too happy to oblige, and made sure that Grant told his leading lady, 'I'm too old for you' and 'I'm old enough to be

your father.' For the woman who had set her sights on Grant, Donen had cast the inimitable Audrey Hepburn. Fragile yet intensely feminine, she had won an Academy Award in her first Hollywood picture, *Roman Holiday*, in 1953, and had almost starred alongside Grant the following year when Paramount wanted him to make *Sabrina*. In *Charade* she was to play a translator who returns home to find her husband murdered and turns to Grant for help. Filming started in October 1962.

Hepburn, thirty-three to Grant's fifty-eight, later described her co-star as 'a mystic' and 'vulnerable', adding that she found an 'indefinable quality' to him which made him 'both expressive and reserved'. His pernickety behaviour on the set had certainly not disappeared, however. He still questioned each one of his lines and argued vehemently that he should not have to do too much 'exposition'. But his professionalism never deserted him once the cameras were running. One scene called for him to take an orange from underneath a stout lady's neck using only his own head and neck. 'It was one of my favourites,' he said later. 'I did it with such concentration that it looked like my life depended on it.' It was filmed on the day that President Kennedy blockaded Cuba, bringing the world to the brink of war.

Exactly as Cary Grant had planned that it should, Stanley Donen's new film burnished his screen image still further. Audrey Hepburn's passion for him on camera almost equalled Grace Kelly's eight years earlier in *To Catch a Thief*. Once again he was the object of a woman's desire. Not many other men

nearing sixty would have Hepburn suggesting to them, 'Won't you come in for a minute? I don't bite, you know, unless it's called for.'

Charade became the twenty-sixth Cary Grant film to play New York's Radio City Music Hall. It opened there in December 1963, and once more it gave the audience the man the *New Yorker*'s critic Pauline Kael described as appearing 'in radiantly shallow perfection'. *Newsweek* called the film 'an absolute delight', complimenting it for 'civilized and witty fun'. But not every critic was as generous. Bosley Crowther in *The New York Times* warned, 'Mr Grant does everything from taking a shower without removing his suit to fighting with thugs with all the blandness and boredom of an old screwball comedy hand.' But that carping did nothing to affect the film's success. In its first week *Charade* took more than $180,000 at Radio City, a house record, and went on to gross more than $6 million in the United States alone.

The moment the film was released Grant left for Europe, to visit his mother. She was eighty-seven now, and her doctors doubted whether she should continue to live alone in the house that he had bought for her in Bristol. But when they met, she acted as she had always done, friendly one moment, criticizing him for his grey hair and wrinkles the next. He would never complain, accepting the criticism like a child, sitting quietly beside her. Age had not made her any more affectionate, it had not warmed the chill that seemed to colour her attitude to the world. Elsie Leach, who was now to be moved into a nursing home, still frightened her son. As it had always been, his refuge was in the character he had created for the screen.

Back in Hollywood shortly after his sixtieth birthday, however, Cary Grant began to wonder how much longer he could realistically remain a leading man. Certainly when Jack Warner approached him to play Professor Higgins in the screen version of the Lerner and Loewe musical *My Fair Lady*, he hesitated. The part would allow him to age on the screen, but he was not sure he would be able to make it a Cary Grant role. Finally, after a long period of thought,

IN ONE OF *CHARADE*'S MOST FAMOUS SCENES, GRANT TOOK A SHOWER IN HIS SUIT. HE ONLY CHANGED INTO A BATH ROBE AFTER SHOOTING WAS OVER.

he turned it down, even though Warner was offering him Audrey Hepburn as his co-star again and was prepared to pay him $1.5 million. 'No matter how good I am,' he said firmly, 'I'll either be compared with Rex Harrison, and I don't think I am better than he is, or I'll be told I'm imitating him, which isn't good for him, or for me.'

Whatever his fears about ageing on the screen, in private he was increasingly besotted with twenty-five-year-old Dyan Cannon. He had paid for her to fly back to Hollywood at weekends while she was in the touring version of *How to Succeed in Business without Really Trying*, and in April 1964 he persuaded her to leave the cast altogether and move into his house in Beverly Hills with him.

Not that he was considering getting married again. 'He didn't want to,' Cannon said later. 'He thought if we did it would ruin our relationship.' Instead he took to making lists of Hollywood's older stars who had relationships with younger women, and showing them to her triumphantly, to prove that age did not matter.

Finally, he decided to experiment with a part that would allow his age to show through on the screen. He told MGM that he might be interested in playing the ageing poker player in a film they were preparing from Ring Lardner and Terry Southern's screenplay *The Cincinnati Kid*, but at the last moment he changed his mind and decided instead to make a film of his own to alter his

GRANT WANTED AUDREY HEPBURN TO BE HIS CO-STAR IN *FATHER GOOSE* FOR UNIVERSAL IN 1964, BUT SHE WAS COMMITTED TO *MY FAIR LADY*. LESLIE CARON ABLY REPLACED HER.

image. Peter Stone, his screenwriter on *Charade*, had come up with an idea which called for him to play an elderly history professor who decides to become a bum on a South Pacific island during the Second World War, only to be persuaded to look out for Japanese planes and troops for the Allies. His character was to be an eccentric with a passion for alcohol: instead of a dinner jacket and a smooth smile, Cary Grant was to wear a work shirt and several days' growth of beard. The idea

WITH GREY HAIR AND A BEARD RATHER THAN HIS USUAL DARKLY POLISHED SMILE, GRANT HOPED *FATHER GOOSE* WOULD HELP HIM TO AGE GRACEFULLY ON THE SCREEN. BUT THE CRITICS HATED HIM AS A BUM.

appealed to him enormously. 'That's what I'm really like,' he told Stone enthusiastically. 'It'll be the first time I've ever appeared as I really am.' Stone suggested the film's title: *Father Goose*.

Grant's first choice for a co-star was Audrey Hepburn, but she was committed to *My Fair Lady*, and he turned instead to a young actress who looked uncannily like her, Leslie Caron. As slight and gamine as Hepburn, Caron had just been nominated for an Academy Award for her performance in *The L-Shaped Room*, and when she and Grant met she was captivated, describing him as 'like a jaguar, ready to pounce... exactly as he is on the screen, only more so'. Once again, Grant decided that Universal could release the film, and he asked Robert Arthur to produce it. He and Arthur then chose Ralph Nelson as director, and decided that the location should be Jamaica rather than the South Pacific. Grant wanted the film to be ready for Radio City Music Hall that Christmas.

When shooting began in April 1964, the French-born Caron found her co-star a mass of contradictions, in the best of moods one moment, but given to sudden flashes of anger. 'He electrified the set,' she said later. 'It was essential to have a quality far above the average. You had

to be as bright and brilliant as possible.' Ever attentive to every detail, Grant took as much interest in the musical score as he did in the performances, choosing Cy Coleman to compose the music and encouraging him to write one particular song for the picture, 'Pass Me By'. He wanted the film to add an extra dimension to his career, to prove that he could age gracefully — and convincingly. His only fear was that it would fail.

In spite of his anxiety, the experiment worked. The cinema audience loved him in jeans and a beard, and they did not mind at all that he had become an unkempt beach bum. In its first week at Radio City in December 1964, *Father Goose* broke *Charade*'s record, taking more than $210,000, and it went on to take another $6 million in film rentals in the United States alone. The critics, however, did not care for Grant as a bum. Brendan Gill noted sourly in the *New Yorker*, '*Father Goose* offers us a surly, slatternly, unshaven and hard-drinking Cary Grant in a part that would have suited Bogart to a T but suits Mr Grant only to about a J.' Bosley Crowther in *The New York Times* suggested that Grant's was 'not a very deep character or a very real one'. Nevertheless the film went on to win Stone and Frank Tarloff an Oscar for the screenplay.

THE TWENTY-SIX-YEAR-OLD
DYAN CANNON BECAME THE
FOURTH MRS GRANT IN JULY
1965. NOW SIXTY-ONE, HE
HAD BEGUN WEARING THE
GLASSES HE CAME TO DEPEND
ON IN PUBLIC.

Just five months later, on Saturday 22 July 1965 a Justice of the Peace in Las Vegas pronounced Cary Grant and Dyan Cannon man and wife. Only a dozen people were present, each one of them sworn to secrecy. Grant did not intend anyone to know that he had married for a fourth time until he had told his mother. As soon as the six-minute ceremony and a brief party afterwards were over, he and Cannon set off for Bristol. But his plan backfired. News of the wedding broke while they were flying across the Atlantic, and when they arrived in England they were besieged by reporters. In desperation, Grant and Cannon climbed out of their hotel room windows at three o'clock in the morning to escape the press. Over the next two days, they managed not only to avoid the reporters, but also to see Mrs Leach.

The fourth Mr and Mrs Grant had hardly settled back into his house in Beverly Hills in August when Dyan announced that she was pregnant. Cary Grant was overjoyed. After years of heart-searching with Barbara Hutton and Betsy Drake over whether or not to start a family, the young woman whom he had married only a matter of weeks before was suddenly to become the mother of his first child. The pregnancy was the sign he had been looking for. Within a month, he had decided to retire. He would make one more picture,

Sadly, the box-office success of *Father Goose* did not satisfy Cary Grant. He had wanted his performance to be a spectacular success with the critics as well as the audience, and the reviews only served to feed his insecurity. The critics put into words what he had privately feared, that the audience did not really want Cary Grant in anything except a Cary Grant film playing a Cary Grant part. Ignoring the film's enormous commercial success, he convinced himself that he had failed to make the transition to character actor that

Bogart had made in *The African Queen*. In his own mind he had not managed to shake off the persona of Cary Grant.

Early in 1965, he was back in England, this time accompanied by Dyan Cannon, whom his mother insisted on addressing as 'Betsy'. Cannon thought that Elsie Leach had 'a psyche that had the strength of a twenty-mule team', and was in no doubt that she could still intimidate her son. Cannon knew that Grant would not consider marrying again if his mother did not approve. To her relief, Elsie Leach rather liked her.

but then he would devote himself to a role he had never played before — husband and father. *Father Goose* had convinced him that he would never be allowed to age on the screen, and he did not want to play a romantic lead any longer, it was not 'believable'. No, he would retire as Garbo had done, and slip quietly away, leaving behind the golden image that he had created.

There was just one last project. Grant had already agreed to remake George Stevens's romantic comedy *The*

More the Merrier, which had been nominated for an Oscar as Best Picture in 1943 when it had starred Jean Arthur and Joel McCrea. The story of a young woman who decides to share her apartment with two men, only to fall in love with the younger one, it had originally been set in Washington, but Columbia wanted to change its location to Tokyo during the Olympic Games. Grant was to play an English industrialist, Sir William Rutland, who is unable to find a room in the city

until he meets a young British Embassy secretary. *Walk Don't Run*, as the remake was to be called, was to be written by Sol Saks and directed by the veteran Charles Walters. Grant's co-stars were to be Samantha Eggar and Jim Hutton, but, at his insistence, he was

Father Goose had convinced Grant that the audience did not want him to grow old on the screen. *Walk Don't Run* in 1966, with Jim Hutton, became his last movie.

ON THE VERGE OF BECOMING
A FATHER FOR THE FIRST TIME,
AT THE AGE OF SIXTY-TWO,
GRANT URGED HIS LEADING
LADY ON *WALK DON'T RUN*,
SAMANTHA EGGAR, TO TAKE
SPECIAL CARE OF HER OWN
NEW BABY.

not going to end up getting the girl. Instead, Grant was to arrange for her marriage to the young American athlete, played by Hutton. 'I honestly think that young people, who are the bulk of the movie-going public, prefer young men to make love to young women,' he told the columnist Sheilah Graham before filming began in October 1965.

Like Leslie Caron, Samantha Eggar, who had just given birth to her first child, was fascinated by her co-star. 'Cary insisted that I had to change my hair, and he chose my dress just as he bought his own props. He was on top of everything.' But she too realized that he seldom revealed much about himself. 'He really didn't open up personally at all, even though I was a friend of Dyan's.' Cannon had opted to stay at home in California for her pregnancy, so what spare time Grant had was spent with Japanese industrialists, such as the President of Sony.

As soon as filming was finished in Tokyo, however, he took off for Los Angeles. He had hardly had time to unpack before Dyan felt the first labour pains. On the morning of 26 February 1966, he ushered his wife into the car and drove her to St John's Hospital in Burbank. At eight that evening Cannon gave birth to a four pound eight ounce baby girl. Within hours, a jubilant Cary

Grant had announced that she would be called Jennifer. 'If she wants another name, she can add it herself.'

From that moment on, Grant's fascination with the business of making movies was replaced by a fascination with his new daughter. He became as obsessed with the details of her upbringing as he had been with the details of his own scripts and sets. He would visit her room at 7.30 each morning, to supervise the warming of her bottle. He would be sure to be back from editing *Walk Don't Run* in time to see her at the end of the day, and to put her to bed. 'She is my greatest production. The most winsome, captivating girl I've ever known,' he told the *Los Angeles Times*. Even the launch of his last film hardly concerned him. When it opened in July 1966, Cary Grant was more interested in taking his daughter to England to see his mother than in the first weekend's takings at the box-office. He set off for England on the liner *Oriana* only days after the opening. As he and Dyan walked up the gangway, he was holding Jennifer. It was the first time he had allowed his daughter to be photographed.

Walk Don't Run did not match the commercial success of *Charade*, but it underlined Grant's enduring appeal. 'Mr Grant has never looked handsomer or in finer fettle,' the *New Yorker* commented, while *Newsweek* added he 'could not be unfunny if he tried'. But the magazine went on to echo his own feelings: 'Though Grant's personal presence is indispensable, the character he plays is almost wholly superfluous. Perhaps the inference to be taken is that a man in his 50s or 60s has no place in romantic

LEFT: 'MY GREATEST
PRODUCTION' – GRANT'S
DAUGHTER JENNIFER.
RIGHT: SHOWING HER OFF
TO HIS EIGHTY-NINE-YEAR-
OLD MOTHER ON A VISIT
TO BRISTOL WITH
DYAN CANNON IN
SEPTEMBER 1966.

to improve his temper. By the time she got back to Hollywood in November, Dyan Cannon was convinced their marriage could not survive.

Three days after Christmas, and barely seventeen months after their wedding, Cannon and Grant separated. She took Jennifer and moved out of their house. 'Cary is a very demanding man,' Cannon was to explain later. 'In a peculiar way, he's such a perfectionist, and has such strong ideas of his own about everything — even about things that women are ordinarily concerned with — that he meddles in what should be women's work.' They had only been apart for a few days, however, when Grant tried to persuade his wife to try again. 'The thought of being separated from your child is intolerable,' he told his friends. 'I don't want to miss a bit of her.' He started telephoning Cannon several times a day, insisting that they had 'to stay together for Jennifer's sake'. But his wife was adamant. 'When there's dissension and heartache in the house you stay apart. Otherwise it's just a cop-out.'

Cary Grant was not to be deterred. He offered to start work again, if Cannon would appear with him, providing she brought Jennifer home. Cannon refused, and accepted a part in a play in New York instead. But when she and her

comedy except as a catalyst.' In fact, Cary Grant had already settled into the only role he intended to play in future: the doting father.

'I retired when I became a father because I didn't want to miss any part of my daughter's growing up,' he was to say later. 'I could have gone on acting and playing a grandfather or a bum, but I discovered more important things in life.' But that did not leave a great deal of room for his wife. Dyan Cannon was quickly made to feel almost irrelevant as

a mother. Indeed her life with Grant had not turned out to be at all what she had expected. Even before Jennifer's birth, he had not liked her going out in the evenings, preferring, as he had always done, to eat in front of the television and clip articles that interested him from the newspapers. Like Betsy Drake, Dyan had discovered the rapid swings of mood that could overtake him, and their trip to England together had done nothing to help. Seeing his mother and introducing her to her first grandchild had done little

daughter turned up to catch the flight, she found he had booked a seat on the same plane. When they checked into their hotel, she found he had booked a suite down the corridor. When she went out to dinner, leaving Jennifer with a nanny, Grant would mysteriously turn up to 'keep an eye on you'. Cannon was furious. But for the next nine months Grant stayed in New York to be within sight of his daughter.

In September 1967, Dyan Cannon's initial petition for divorce came before the Los Angeles Domestic Relations Court. Her lawyers claimed that she needed a maintenance payments of $5,470 a month, and insisted that her

husband could well afford it as his annual income was $500,000, and he was worth at least $10 million. Neither she nor Grant was in court, however. She was still appearing on Broadway, and he was nearby, staying at a friend's apartment. Their arguments raged on throughout the winter. She wanted a divorce. He tried to persuade her to think again. She refused, insisting that if he would not accept her terms she would tell the world exactly how difficult life had been for Mrs Cary Grant.

A week before Cannon was due to make her first appearance in court, Grant was hurt in an accident on the way to the airport to return to Los

Angeles for the hearing. Forced to remain in hospital, he was not in the Santa Monica Superior Court in March 1968 to hear his wife explain that living with him had turned into 'a terrifying, unromantic nightmare'. Sparing not a single detail, Cannon told the court that Grant had not only beaten her up but also regularly locked her in her room, because he was given to 'fits of uncontrollable temper'. When her

A HOLLYWOOD LEGEND, GRANT ADMIRED ACTORS OF THE NEW GENERATION, SUCH AS PAUL NEWMAN, HERE WITH HIS WIFE JOANNE WOODWARD ON THE SET OF *WINNING*.

lawyer asked if she could explain his behaviour, she answered, 'I attribute it to LSD', and then explained that he had been taking it for ten years and had 'suggested I try it'. Cannon's catalogue of her husband's failings did not end there. The next morning she added that he would 'yell and scream and jump up and down', and that, during the Academy Awards on television, he had become particularly violent. 'I couldn't please him, no matter what I'd do or say,' she went on. 'He criticized everything I did — the way I carried the baby, the way I dressed the baby. I couldn't do anything right.' It was some of the most damaging public criticism ever levelled against a movie star.

To rebut Cannon's evidence, Cary Grant's lawyers called two psychiatrists to prove that although he had taken LSD it had caused no 'organic defects' in his brain, and that 'there are no irrational effects to prevent him from being a loving father or to make him endanger his daughter'. In a final statement, his lawyers explained, 'He, at the age of sixty-four, wants to devote the rest of his life to making his daughter happy.' Judge Robert Wenke was impressed. He saw no reason to deny Grant reasonable access to his daughter, however much LSD he may have taken in the past. The judge ruled that he should be allowed to see Jennifer 'sixty days of each year' and to keep her overnight at reasonable times.

When Grant left hospital in New York, a few days later, he flew directly to Los Angeles in a private jet owned by George Barrie, the founder of the Fabergé cosmetics company, whom he

had just met. On the flight across the United States, Barrie suggested that Grant should become a director of his company and act as 'a sort of informal ambassador for us'. For his part, Grant was fascinated by the intense little man, who had started life playing the saxophone for a living. Seven weeks later, to the amazement of Hollywood, he became a director of Fabergé, and over the next decade he and Barrie were to become close friends. Fabergé

OUT OF 'THE PICTURE BUSI-
NESS', GRANT INCREASINGLY
DEVOTED HIS TIME TO THE
FABERGÉ COMPANY, EVEN TO
THE EXTENT OF MODELLING
THEIR CLOTHES.

became his new 'studio', and the company provided him with a private plane, expenses and a small annual fee, as well as stock options. It was an association that was to last for the next eighteen years. 'Somehow,' one friend admitted

Now in his mid-sixties, but hardly looking it, Grant was immensely proud to have been part of what he called 'Hollywood's most glorious era'.

later, 'Cary seemed to think the life of a businessman was more respectable — or admirable — than acting.'

Not that the film offers stopped coming. Throughout 1968 and 1969, every Hollywood studio tried to persuade Cary Grant to return to the screen. But he steadfastly refused them all. He did not want to risk losing touch with Jennifer, and in October 1969 he even managed to persuade the court to revise the visiting arrangements. Now his daughter was to be allowed to stay with him on alternate weekends from Friday evening until Sunday afternoon, as well as every Monday afternoon from three until six. She was also to be allowed to stay for half the Christmas holidays, all the Easter holidays in alternate years, and for one month of each summer holiday. It was all he wanted. There was simply no time to make another film.

In the first months of 1970 Hollywood itself recognized that Cary Grant had brought his career to an end. On 7 April the Academy of Motion Picture Arts and Sciences finally gave him an Oscar. The citation for his special honorary award read, 'To Cary Grant for his unique mastery of the art of screen acting with the respect and affection of his colleagues.' The gold statuette was presented to Grant by Frank Sinatra, who said simply, 'It was awarded for sheer brilliance of acting....

No one has brought more pleasure to more people for many years than Cary has, and nobody has done so many things so well. Cary has so much skill that it makes it all look easy.' The applause was thunderous, and the tears in Cary Grant's eyes were only too clear.

His voice was almost a whisper as he started to speak. 'Probably no greater honour can come to a man than the respect of his colleagues,' he said. 'You know I may never look at this without remembering the quiet patience of the directors who were so kind to me, who

were kind enough to put up with me more than once — some of them even three or four times.... Well, I trust they and all the other directors, writers and producers, and leading women, have all forgiven me what I didn't know.' As the audience rose to its feet to give him a standing ovation, he concluded, 'You know, I've never been a joiner or a member of any — of a particular — social set, but I've been privileged to be a part of Hollywood's most glorious era.'

It was Cary Grant's last Hollywood performance.

CHAPTER EIGHT · JENNIFER AND BARBARA

Like Garbo before him, Cary Grant slipped out of pictures and took refuge in his privacy. For most of the remaining years of his life, producer after producer, studio after studio, would send him scripts or suggestions for movies that he might make. But he would politely refuse them all.

George Barrie of Fabergé even created a film production company with him in mind. One of Barrie's first scripts, *A Touch of Class*, in 1972, Grant turned down without a moment's hesitation, telling his friend, 'If the script had been given to me ten years ago I'd have made it in a second.' The role went to George Segal, thirty years Grant's junior.

In the same year, another old friend, Joe Mankiewicz, tried to persuade him to play the lead in the film version of Anthony Shaffer's stage play, *Sleuth*, but again Grant declined. When MGM asked him if he would play John Barrymore's role in a remake of *Grand Hotel*, once again he said no. In the last sixteen years of his life, Cary Grant's only real interest was Jennifer. The man who been denied a childhood himself was intent on ensuring that his daughter

was not denied one. Nothing was to be allowed to interfere.

It was the reason Grant wanted to help Dyan Cannon get her career started again. The more time she spent on set making a film, the more time he would be allowed with Jennifer. Shortly after their divorce he had suggested she should be considered for Columbia's film *Bob and Carol and Ted and Alice*, and the studio had agreed. But eventually his attempts to help his ex-wife were to lead to a new public battle between them. In March 1972, Dyan agreed to appear in *Shamus* opposite Burt Reynolds, and decided to take Jennifer with her to New York for the filming, even though Jennifer had only just started at the Montessori School in Malibu. Grant was enraged, and seized the opportunity to ask the Los Angeles court for joint custody of his daughter, so that when his wife went away for long periods she could stay with him. After another bitter courtroom argument, the court ruled that six-year-old Jennifer Grant should remain in California, but that her father should take her to New York for at least two visits during her mother's filming. Cary Grant was jubilant.

When he was not looking after his daughter, however, he occupied his time much as he had done in the past. He

'Women are instinctively wiser and emotionally more mature than men.'

TWO WOMEN WERE TO PLAY A VITAL PART IN THE LAST YEARS OF GRANT'S LIFE: HIS FIFTH WIFE BARBARA HARRIS (LEFT) AND HIS DAUGHTER JENNIFER (ABOVE RIGHT).

RIGHT: HIS ATTRACTION TO
BEAUTIFUL WOMEN HAD
NEVER DIMMED, AND IN THE
EARLY 1970S GRANT
EMBARKED ON A RELATION-
SHIP WITH A YOUNG BRITISH
PHOTOGRAPHER, MAUREEN
DONALDSON.

would attend to his investments and
reply to correspondence during the
morning, and in the afternoon would
either stay at home or go to the races at
Hollywood Park. If he placed a bet,
however, it would never be more than
$2, for he was still as careful with his
money as he had always been. Shortly
after winning the right for Jennifer to
spend more time with him in California,
he sold the rights to some of his last
films with Universal, including
Operation Petticoat, *That Touch of
Mink*, *The Grass Is Greener* and
Charade, for $2 million and invested the
money in property, including one
development in southern Spain and
another in Ireland. He travelled to
Europe with George Barrie for Fabergé,
and went to Las Vegas from time to
time as a new director of MGM, but
Jennifer was his consuming passion.

Not that he had lost his appetite for
the company of pretty young women. In
1971, he embarked on an affair with
Maureen Donaldson, a young reporter
turned photographer, and in the middle
of 1972 she went to live with him in
Beverly Hills. But the contradictions in
his personality had not disappeared.
'The dark and the light live side by side
in Cary Grant,' Donaldson wrote later,
suggesting that his mother's desertion of
him as a child had instilled a distrust of
women that he had never shaken off.

She sensed the ambivalence that perme-
ated his life: a desire for privacy, and yet
'not wishing to be forgotten'; a fortune
of many millions of dollars, 'which he
would never let himself enjoy'; a distaste
for talking about the past but an archive

of memorabilia in his house. Donaldson
agreed with Pauline Kael that Grant
'drew women to him by making them
feel he needed them, yet the last thing
he'd do would be to come right out and
say it'. Kael was describing his screen

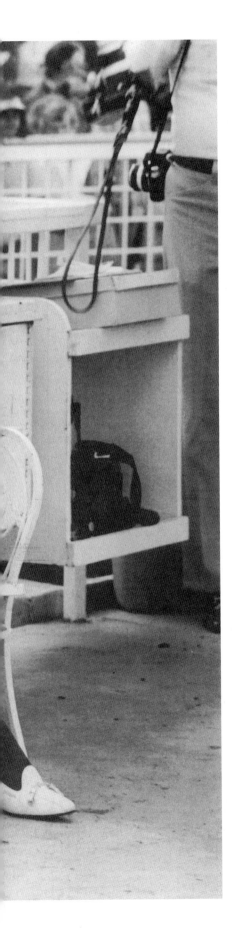

LEFT: DURING THEIR FIVE-
YEAR AFFAIR, GRANT AND
MAUREEN DONALDSON
OFTEN WENT HORSE-RACING
AT HOLLYWOOD PARK.
RIGHT: A PORTRAIT TAKEN
BY DONALDSON.

appearances, but Donaldson insisted the same was true of his private life.

On 22 January 1973, just two weeks before her ninety-sixth birthday, Elsie Leach died in her Bristol nursing home. She fell asleep after being given her afternoon tea and never recovered consciousness. Two days later, her only son went back to the town of his birth and buried her alongside the other man she had never made happy, his father Elias. They had hardly been together during their life, but Grant wanted to reunite them in death.

Even in her last years, Elsie Leach had found it impossible to accept her son's success. 'One time I took her some fur coats,' Grant once recalled. 'And I remember she said, 'What do you want from me now?' I said, 'It's just because I love you.' And she said something like, 'Oh you...' She wouldn't accept it.' It took Grant six months to gather up the courage to clear out his mother's house in Bristol. 'To do it sooner,' he said, 'would have seemed like hurrying her away.'

Grant eventually took his mother's belongings back with him to Hollywood and stored them in a fireproof vault which had been specially constructed in his house. Here he kept meticulous records of his past, photographs of his parents and his friends, details of his life in vaudeville and on Broadway, his old marriage certificates and divorce papers,

passports and press cuttings, contracts and publicity stills, posters and lobby cards, together with presents from Noël Coward and Cole Porter. All were neatly stacked, often tied together in rubber bands. There he put his mother's rings beside his father's pocket watch.

On Jennifer's eleventh birthday in February 1977, Grant wrote to her to tell her how proud he was to be able to watch her swim, ride and play tennis. 'You are the dearest daughter a man could have,' he wrote. 'You have never caused me a moment's anguish or disappointment.' When Warren Beatty approached him later that year to play the part of the ghost in a remake of the 1940 classic *Here Comes Mr Jordan*, which Beatty wanted to retitle *Heaven*

Right: With the pressures of making pictures behind him, Grant relaxed and allowed himself to indulge his passion for horses, sometimes taking his daughter Jennifer along.

Can Wait, Grant again turned the idea down. Movies were things of the past.

Cary Grant's retirement was not a desperate search for seclusion, however. He did not hide behind sunglasses and try to avoid the photographers, as Garbo did. He still did not care for crowds, and had the same aversion to autograph hunters that he had always had, but he was happy enough to visit MGM's

hotels, go to Fabergé sales conferences and turn up for board meetings at the Norton Simon Museum and the Hollywood Park racecourse.

He was also not anxious to be alone. His relationship with Maureen Donaldson, which had lasted for almost four years, was gradually to be replaced with another. On a trip to London for Fabergé in 1976, he was introduced to Barbara Harris, a young public relations officer working at the Royal Lancaster Hotel. Born in Dar es Salaam in September 1950, the brown-haired and brown-eyed Harris was one of three daughters of a much decorated army officer. Though he was forty-six years

older than she was, Grant was beguiled by the calm young woman, who delighted in driving him round London in her Mini.

Over the next two years, Cary Grant kept in constant touch with Barbara Harris, sending her flowers and telephoning her almost every day; as his interest in her grew, so his relationship with Donaldson gradually drew to a close. When he travelled to England, he took care to spend as much time as he could with Harris, and regularly invited her to visit him in California, although she always refused. But in June 1978, Grant invited her to join him in the South of France, where he was to be a

ON A TRIP TO LONDON FOR FABERGÈ IN 1977 (*ABOVE*), GRANT MET BARBARA HARRIS, THE YOUNG LONDON PUBLIC RELATIONS OFFICER WHO WAS TO BECOME HIS FIFTH WIFE (*RIGHT*).

guest at the wedding of Princess Caroline of Monaco. To his delight, she agreed, and soon afterwards she went to California with him for a three-week visit. The person above any other whom Cary Grant wanted Barbara Harris to meet was his daughter Jennifer.

The two young women, one just twelve, the other twenty-eight, could almost have been sisters. Both had wide open smiles and wore their brown hair

GRANT FINALLY PLUCKED UP
THE COURAGE TO ASK
BARBARA HARRIS TO MARRY
HIM IN APRIL 1981, FOUR
YEARS AFTER THEIR RELATION-
SHIP HAD BEGUN. HE WAS
FORTY-SIX YEARS HER SENIOR.

organize their trips, and allow her to look after him.

But the passing years brought the death of many of his friends. In 1976, Howard Hughes, whom he had hardly seen in almost a decade, and had spoken to on the telephone only from time to time, died a recluse in Texas. The same year his friend and former co-star Rosalind Russell succumbed to cancer, and the following year brought the death of their director in *His Girl Friday*, Howard Hawks. In the summer of 1979, Lord Mountbatten, another friend, was killed in a terrorist bombing, and a year later Alfred Hitchcock died at the age of eighty-one.

Finally, at the age of seventy-seven, Grant plucked up the courage to marry again. The first person he confided in was his daughter. 'When I first told Jennifer that I was going to marry Barbara,' he said later, 'her eyes filled with tears. For a moment I thought she was upset. She was just the opposite. She was thrilled for me.' He told her, 'For goodness sake, don't say anything to Barbara, I might not have the courage to ask her.' But on 11 April 1981, Cary Grant did indeed marry Barbara Harris on the verandah of his Hollywood home, watched by his daughter Jennifer, then aged fifteen. As soon as the ceremony was over, the fifth Mrs Cary Grant led the small group of witnesses inside the house for a wedding lunch

drawn back from their foreheads. They liked each other at once. Within a few weeks of her first trip to California, Harris had given up her job in London and moved into Grant's house in Beverly Hills. 'I was absolutely terrified of the age difference,' she admitted afterwards. 'But I decided to go through with it because, otherwise, you don't enjoy the time you do have, which is precious.'

Barbara Harris brought Cary Grant a serenity that he had never experienced before. One friend explained later, 'It was only when he met Barbara that he found what he had been searching for: the everyday happiness that lasted all day, all night, day after day, month after month, year after year.' She also brought order to his life. It was her efforts that saw the workmen finally complete the redevelopment of his house, with its wing for Jennifer, with which he had been struggling for six years. She too who managed to persuade him to let her

she had prepared herself. She had not hired a caterer, she explained, because, 'we didn't want to let our secret out'. Nor were they anxious for the world to know. It was to be almost eight days before anyone discovered. By that time the new Mr and Mrs Cary Grant were staying with Frank and Barbara Sinatra on their estate in Palm Springs, where

THE NEW MRS CARY GRANT WITH HER EIGHTEEN-YEAR-OLD STEPDAUGHTER JENNIFER AND HER HUSBAND AT A CHARITY DINNER IN LOS ANGELES IN 1984.

Grace Kelly and Prince Rainier were holding their twenty-fifth wedding anniversary celebrations.

Cary Grant's life hardly changed after the wedding. He and Barbara would stay at home most of the time with their two cats, swimming occasionally and sitting on their patio looking out across Los Angeles. On most weekdays, they would have a light lunch together on the verandah after he had finished on the telephone. In the afternoons, he would sunbathe while she gardened, and they would

practise French together before tea. As dusk fell they would play backgammon, card games or Trivial Pursuit, and then have dinner in front of the television. At the weekends, she would cook for him.

If they went out, it was usually only to a charity dinner, to Hollywood Park or Dodger Stadium, although he would sometimes take her to the Magic Castle, a magician's club just off Hollywood Boulevard. They would drive to Palm Springs for the weekend and return to England regularly to allow her to see her mother in Devon. For her part, Barbara

TO HER FATHER'S DELIGHT,
JENNIFER GRANT STUDIED AT
STANFORD UNIVERSITY IN
SAN FRANCISCO (*LEFT*). BUT
NOTHING COULD RELIEVE HIS
SADNESS AT THE SUDDEN
DEATH OF GRACE KELLY IN
1982 (*ABOVE*).

Grant made clothes for everyone. She knitted pullovers for Jennifer and sewed brightly coloured shirts for her husband, which he wore over white trousers with only slippers or sandals on his feet. She also made caftans for them both, which he took great delight in wearing — to the astonishment of some of his friends.

Only a year after his fifth marriage, Cary Grant's two favourite leading ladies died within a few months of each other. Grace Kelly was killed in a car accident on the French Riviera and Ingrid Bergman died of cancer. The sense of a passing era, which he had mentioned at the Oscar ceremony in 1970, was gathering pace, though somehow he never seemed part of it. Not for one moment did he look or seem almost eighty. His hair may have turned white, and his skin wrinkled with the years, but in the words of one friend, 'Cary never became an old man.'

Grant may not have made a film for more than fifteen years, but he was not forgotten. His friends the Reagans invited him to the White House in the autumn of 1981, and two months later he was back in Washington to be honoured at the Kennedy Centre for his lifelong contribution to the cinema. At MGM

RECOGNIZED FOR HIS LIFE-LONG CONTRIBUTION TO THE MOTION-PICTURE INDUSTRY, GRANT ACCEPTED THE GOLDEN LION AWARD AT THE AGE OF EIGHTY.

the studio named their largest preview theatre after him, provoking him to remark that no one had ever named anything after him — 'except my mother, who once called her dog Archie'. Shortly afterwards, Hollywood Park named a pavilion in his honour.

Barbara Grant slowly encouraged her husband to accept the affection that so many people felt for him. She gently persuaded him to consider the offers he was getting to talk about his life, and in particular one from Nancy Nelson, who ran a New York lecture bureau. It was Nelson, with Barbara's assistance, who cajoled Grant into giving the first of what were eventually to become thirty-six public appearances called 'Evenings with Cary Grant', in which he would sit on a stool in the centre of the stage

answering questions from the audience. For a man who had spent his life trying to conceal himself from the world, and had refused an offer of $5 million to write his autobiography, it was a remarkable change of heart. In October 1984, he suffered a mild stroke, but went on with the lecture series nevertheless. The knowledge that vast numbers of cinema-goers and movie-lovers had not forgotten him, even at the age of eighty, seemed both to surprise and to delight him. As the series progressed, he refined the lectures, introducing each evening with an eight-minute montage of his films, but he never once prepared a speech, and refused to have any questions planted in the audience. The years in vaudeville, watching the comics from the wings, had not forsaken him. He still liked to ad-lib.

It was while Cary Grant was preparing for one of these evenings, in Davenport, Iowa, that he was taken ill. Complaining of a headache and feeling sick, he left the technical rehearsal shortly after five o'clock to go back to his hotel suite. Two hours later he was rushed into intensive care at St Luke's Hospital after suffering a massive stroke At 11.22 in the evening of Saturday 29 November 1986 Cary Grant died at the age of eighty-two.

Ronald Reagan was among the first to pay tribute to his friend's talent: 'His elegance, wit and charm will endure forever on film and in our hearts.' Eva

Marie Saint described him as 'the most handsome, witty and stylish leading man, both on and off the screen', and Elizabeth Taylor compared him to a 'great fireplace.... He warmed you and made you feel super. He was what one would hope a movie star would be like.' Alexis Smith, his co-star in *Night and Day*, called him 'the best movie actor that ever was', adding, 'There's a term 'romance with a camera' and I don't think anybody ever had as great a 'romance with the camera' as he did.' In *The New York Times*, Vincent Canby suggested that 'like Cole Porter melodies, he seems simply to have happened', while in the *Los Angeles Times* Charles Champlin described him as 'the supreme romantic figure.... There was never anyone else quite like him.'

Cary Grant had become a Hollywood monument. Fay Wray, his co-star in *Nikki* all those years before on Broadway, spoke for most of his colleagues in Hollywood when she said, 'When he died, not only was Cary gone, but an era had disappeared.'

People magazine called him 'the King of Hearts, the mirror of charm, the most glamorous leading man of his generation...the grandmaster of the graceful exit', adding, 'The face alone was overpowering: strong sexy mouth, glittering brown eyes, rotisserie tan, chin-cleft you could crack a nut in. Then there was the whip-taut body, the deft movements, the caressing twang, the what's-it accent. Was he serious? Was he joking? Was the joke on him? On you? You could never be sure. He approached, avoided, dodged definition, baffled — yet always entertained.'

Two weeks later the critic Richard Schickel expanded the point in an eloquent obituary in *Time* magazine. He described Cary Grant as 'a perfectly beautiful man...with a singular style of speech. He is confident without being overbearing, confidential without being intrusive, quite irresistible despite the fact...that he had one of the most imitated voices of the century.' No one, on screen or off, 'had any alternative to bedazzlement as a response to him.... Some distant day,' Schickel suggested, 'audiences may even come to agree with a minority of Grant's contemporaries that he was not merely the greatest movie star of his era, but the medium's subtlest and slyest actor as well.'

The obituary's headline would have appealed to Grant. It read, 'The acrobat of the drawing room'.

So great was the affection felt for Cary Grant in Hollywood that in October 1988, almost two years after his death, a dinner in his honour was held at the Beverly Hilton Hotel, at which more than 940 guests paid $1,000 each in donations to the Princess Grace Foundation, raising almost $1 million to assist young people in theatre, dance and film. The audience included almost every surviving member of Hollywood's aristocracy — among them the Reagans, Sinatras, Stewarts and

IN HIS LAST YEARS, BARBARA ENCOURAGED HER HUSBAND TO PRESENT 'EVENINGS WITH CARY GRANT' THROUGHOUT THE UNITED STATES.

WHEN ASKED IN A TELEGRAM 'HOW OLD CARY GRANT?', HE REPLIED, 'OLD CARY GRANT FINE. HOW YOU?'. THOUGH HE LATER DENIED HAVING SAID IT, NO ONE COULD DENY THAT AT EIGHTY-TWO HE LOOKED AS FINE AS EVER.

just a few weeks after Jennifer Grant had married for the first time, in the early summer of 1993.

In its own memorial the Los Angeles County Museum of Art screened every one of the seventy-two films that Cary Grant had left behind, and called him simply 'the best and most important actor in the history of the cinema'. There was no hint of hyperbole in the title. In each and every one, the man whom the feminist Camille Paglia called 'almost supernatural, a magnificent male animal' shone from the screen, projecting the incandescent image that he had created for the audience to know and love.

As Cary Grant himself put it, 'I pretended to be somebody I wanted to be, and I finally became that person, or he became me. Or we met at some point. It's a relationship.' Although few people outside Hollywood knew it, it was also an act of the most painstaking professionalism, marking him out as one of the cinema's most remarkable actors. 'I've often been accused of being myself on the screen,' he once explained. 'But being oneself on the screen is much more difficult than you would suppose.' No matter how troubled he may have been in private, Cary Grant made it look easy, and by doing so created a screen persona that is unmistakable. A decade after his death, it is a legacy that no one who loves the cinema can ever forget.

Pecks, Robert Mitchum, Sammy Davis, Liza Minnelli and Walter Matthau. Sophia Loren filmed her own tribute, and Deborah Kerr composed a poem in memory of the man she called a friend. It was the only public ceremony that Barbara and Jennifer Grant sanctioned in his memory. There was no public grave. Cary Grant's will had insisted that he be cremated.

His wife and daughter were also to help to preserve his memory in the years after his death. Barbara Grant donated

her husband's papers to the Margaret Herrick Library at the Academy of Motion Picture Arts and Science in Los Angeles, and his daughter followed in his footsteps, first taking acting lessons and then appearing in episodes of the television series *Beverly Hills 90210*. The two women remained friends, and shared the fortune that Grant's caution had amassed — an estimated $80 million. Barbara Grant waited almost seven years after her husband's death before marrying again, doing so

Filmography

1932
This Is the Night
Director: Frank Tuttle
(Paramount Publix)
Sinners in the Sun
Director: Alexander Hall
(Paramount Publix)
Merrily We Go to Hell
Director: Dorothy Arzner
(Paramount Publix)
Devil and the Deep
Director: Marion Gering
(Paramount Publix)
Blonde Venus
Director: Josef von Sternberg
(Paramount Publix)
Hot Saturday
Director: William Seiter
(Paramount Publix)
Madame Butterfly
Director: Marion Gering
(Paramount Publix)

1933
She Done Him Wrong
Director: Lowell Sherman
(Paramount Publix)
Woman Accused
Director: Paul Sloane
(Paramount Publix)
The Eagle and the Hawk
Director: Stuart Walker
(Paramount Publix)
Gambling Ship
Directors: Louis Gasnier
and Max Marcin
(Paramount Publix)
I'm No Angel
Director: Wesley Ruggles
(Paramount Publix)
Alice in Wonderland
Director: Norman Z. McLeod
(Paramount Publix)

1934
Thirty Day Princess
Director: Marion Gering
(Paramount Publix)
Born to Be Bad
Director: Lowell Sherman
(United Artists)
Kiss and Make Up
Director: Harlan Thompson
(Paramount Publix)
Ladies Should Listen
Director: Frank Tuttle
(Paramount Publix)

1935
Enter Madame
Director: Elliott Nugent
(Paramount Publix)
Wings in the Dark
Director: James Flood
(Paramount)
The Last Outpost
Directors: Charles Barton
and Louis Gasnier
(Paramount)

1936
Sylvia Scarlett
Director: George Cukor
(RKO Radio)
Big Brown Eyes
Director: Raoul Walsh
(Paramount)
Suzy
Director: George Fitzmaurice
(MGM)
Wedding Present
Director: Richard Wallace
(Paramount)
 *The Amazing Quest of Ernest
Bliss* (US title, *Romance and
Riches*)
Director: Alfred Zeisler
(Garrett-Klement Pictures)

1937
When You're in Love
(GB title, *For You Alone*)
Director: Robert Riskin
(Columbia)
The Toast of New York
Director: Rowland V. Lee
(RKO Radio)
Topper
Director: Norman Z. McLeod
(MGM)
The Awful Truth
Director: Leo McCarey
(Columbia)

1938
Bringing Up Baby
Director: Howard Hawks
(RKO Radio)
Holiday
(GB titles, *Free to Live*;
Unconventional Linda)
Director: George Cukor
(Columbia)

1939
Gunga Din
Director: George Stevens
(RKO Radio)
Only Angels Have Wings
Director: Howard Hawks
(Columbia)
In Name Only
Director: John Cromwell
(RKO Radio)

1940
His Girl Friday
Director: Howard Hawks
(Columbia)
My Favorite Wife
Director: Garson Kanin
(RKO Radio)
The Howards of Virginia
(GB title, *The Tree of Liberty*)
Director: Frank Lloyd
(Columbia)
The Philadelphia Story
Director: George Cukor
(MGM)

1941
Penny Serenade
Director: George Stevens
(Columbia)
Suspicion
Director: Alfred Hitchcock
(RKO Radio)

1942
The Talk of the Town
Director: George Stevens
(Columbia)
Once Upon a Honeymoon
Director: Leo McCarey
(RKO Radio)

1943
Mr Lucky
Director: H. C. Potter
(RKO Radio)
Destination Tokyo
Director: Delmer Daves
(Warner Brothers)

1944
Once Upon a Time
Director: Alexander Hall
(Columbia)
None but the Lonely Heart
Director: Clifford Odets
(RKO Radio)
Arsenic and Old Lace
Director: Frank Capra
(Warner Brothers)

1946
Night and Day
Director: Michael Curtiz
Warner Brothers
Notorious
Director: Alfred Hitchcock
(RKO Radio)

1947
*The Bachelor and the
Bobby-Soxer*
(GB title, *Bachelor Knight*)
Director: Irving Reis
(A Dore Schary Production)
The Bishop's Wife
Director: Henry Koster
(RKO Radio)

1948
*Mr Blandings Builds His Dream
House*
Director: H. C. Potter
(RKO Radio)
Every Girl Should Be Married
Director: Don Hartman
(RKO Radio)

1949
I Was a Male War Bride
Director: Howard Hawks
(Twentieth Century-Fox)

1950
Crisis
Director: Richard Brooks
(MGM)

1951
People Will Talk
Director: Joseph L. Mankiewicz
(Twentieth Century-Fox)

1952
Room for One More
Director: Norman Taurog
(Warner Brothers)
Monkey Business
Director: Howard Hawks
(Twentieth Century-Fox)

1953
Dream Wife
Director: Sidney Sheldon
(MGM)

1955
To Catch a Thief
Director: Alfred Hitchcock
(Paramount/Alfred Hitchcock)

1957
The Pride and the Passion
Director: Stanley Kramer
(United Artists/Stanley Kramer)
An Affair to Remember
Director: Leo McCarey
(Twentieth Century-Fox)
Kiss Them for Me
Director: Stanley Donen
(Twentieth Century-Fox)

1958
Indiscreet
Director: Stanley Donen
(Warner Brothers)
Houseboat
Director: Mel Shavelson
(Paramount/Scribe)

1959
North by Northwest
Director: Alfred Hitchcock
(MGM)
Operation Petticoat
Director: Blake Edwards
(Universal)

1960
The Grass Is Greener
Director: Stanley Donen
(Universal)

1962
That Touch of Mink
Director: Delbert Mann
(Universal/Granlex/Arwin/
Nob Hill)

1964
Charade
Director: Stanley Donen
(Universal/Stanley Donen)
Father Goose
Director: Ralph Nelson
(Universal)

1966
Walk, Don't Run
Director: Charles Walters
(Columbia)

Index

Page numbers in *italic* refer to illustrations

Academy of Motion Picture
    Arts and Sciences
    Academy Awards 49, 52, 69,
        72, 81, *82*, 91, 103, 119,
        138, 160, 169
    honorary award 171
    Margaret Herrick Library
        188
Adair, Jean 79
Affair to Remember, An 131-2,
    131, 132
Agee, James 89, 110
Alexander, John 79
Alice in Wonderland 34
All About Eve 116
*Amazing Quest of Ernest Bliss,
    The* 41, *42*, 43
American Army Air Corps 82
Anastasia 138
Andrea Doria 130
Anhalt, Edward & Edna 128
Antibes 125
Arnold, Edward 43
*Around the World in Eighty
    Days* 126-8
Arsenic and Old Lace 13, 76-9,
    78, 79, 90
Arthur, Jean 55, *59*, 80, 163
Arthur, Robert 151, 160
Astoria 21
Avery, Stephen Morehouse 110
Awful Truth, The 46, 47-50,
    48-50, 52, 65, 72, 82, 131

*Bachelor and the Bobbysoxer,
    The* 101-3, *103*, 112
Baker, Herbert 119
Bankhead, Tallulah 25, *25*
Barnes, Howard 90
Barrie, George 169, 173, 175
Barry, Philip 52, 64
Barrymore, Ethel 89, *89*, 90-1,
    91
Barrymore, John 76, 89, 173
Barthelmass, Richard 27
Beatty, Warren 177
Bellamy, Ralph 47, 52
Beloved Infidel 151
Bennett, Constance 44, *44-5*
Bennett, Joan 42
Bercovici, Leonardo 104
Bergman, Ingrid *92*, 96-7, 97-9,
    100-1, 136-8, *136-9*, 185
Berman, Pandro 39
Better Times 18
Beverly Hills 71, 136, 159,
    162, 175, 182
Beverly Hills 90210 188
Beverly Hilton Hotel 187
Big Brown Eyes 42
Bishop Road School, Bristol 15
Bishop's Wife, The 104, *105-7*
Blair, Janet 88
Blonde Venus 25, *26*
*Bob and Carol and Ted and
    Alice* 173
Bogart, Humphrey 162
Bogdanovich, Peter 55
Boom, Boom 20
Born to Be Bad 36
Boy on a Dolphin 130
Boyer, Charles 131-2
Brando, Marlon 142
Bridge on the River Kwai, The
    128
Brien, Mary 41

Bringing Up Baby 47, 50-3, *51*,
    119
Briskin, Sam 50
Brisson, Freddie 60, *60*
Bristol 13-17, 41, 88, 101, 104,
    149, *167*, 177
Broadway Melody 20
Brook, Clive 25
Brooks, Phyllis 44, *44*, 57, *57*,
    60, 62-3, 71
Brooks, Richard 115, *115*
Buchanan, Jack 19
Buchman, Sidney 64, 80
Burns, George 18

Camille 52
Canby, Vincent 187
Cannon, Dyan 155, 159, 162,
    162, 164-9, *167*, 173
Capote, Truman 141
Capra, Frank 43, 76-9, *78*
Carmichael, Hoagy *44-5*
Caroline, Princess 180
Caron, Leslie *159*, 160
Carroll, Nancy 29, 31
Casablanca 90
Champlin, Charles 187
Chan, Jackie 150
Chang, Anna *17*
Charade 155, 156-8, *156-8*,
    175
Charig, Phil 21, 27
Charlot, André 19
Cherrill, Virginia 32-5, *34-5*,
    37-8, 71, 142
Chevalier, Maurice 20
Church of Religious Science
    122
Cincinnati Kid, The 159
Citizen Kane 76
City Lights 32
Coburn, Charles 119
Cogan, Alma 150
Cohn, Harry 42, 47, 63, 72,
    80, 103
Colbert, Claudette 59
Coleman, Cy 160
Colman, Ronald 80, *80-1*, 81,
    103
Columbia 42-4, 47, 52-4, 57,
    63, 69, 71, 80-1, 86-7, 103,
    128, 163, 173
Coney Island 18
Cooper, Gary 23, 25, 31, 34,
    37, 63, 81, 111, 128
Coote, Robert *53*
Coward, Noël 19, *33*, 177
Crisis 114, 115-16
Cromwell, John 56, *57*
Crosby, Bing 34, 91
Crowther, Bosley 62, 64, 67,
    88, 90, 99, 112, 119, 126,
    133, 158, 160
Cukor, George 39-41, 52, 64-5,
    65, 67, 69, 121
Curtis, Tony 145
Curtiz, Michael 90, 93-4

Daily Mirror (New York) 72
Damita, Lili 24, *37*
Davenport 186
Daves, Delmer 86
Davis, Bette 76
Dawn Patrol 50
Day, Doris *149*, 153, *154*
Day, Laraine 84-6
Destination Tokyo 86-8, *87*
Devil and the Deep, The 25, *25*
Diamond, I.A.L. 118
Dietrich, Marlene 13, 25, 26-7,
    29
Di Frasso, Dorothy *39*, 57, 63,
    82

Dodge, David 126
Donaldson, Maureen 175-7,
    175-6, 180
Donen, Stanley 67, 133-6, 149,
    155-6
Double Life, A 103
Drake, Betsy 107-10, *111*,
    112-17, *115-17*, 119, 121-2,
    128, 130-1, 133-6, 141-5,
    149-50, 155
Drake, Frances 36
Dream Wife 119, *119*
Duck Soup 47
Dunne, Irene 46, 47-9, 52, 59,
    61-2, *61-2*, 71, 72, 80, 131
du Pont, Mariana 41

Eagle and the Hawk, The 31,
    32
Edwards, Blake 145
Eggar, Samantha 163-4, *164-5*
Empire Theatre, Bristol 16-17
Enter Madam 37
Ephron, Nora 132
Epstein, Jules 133
Epstein, Julius & Philip 79
Esquire 36
'Evenings with Cary Grant'
    186, *187*
Every Girl Should Be Married
    110-11, *111*

Fabergé 169, *169*, 175, 180,
    180
Fairbanks Jr, Douglas 53, *53*,
    84
Fairfield Secondary School 16
Fame magazine 111
Farmer, Frances 43, *43*
Farrow, John 126
Father Goose 159-63, *159*,
    160-1
Ferguson, Harvey 29
Ferguson, Otis 49, 52, 72, 86
Ferrer, José 115
Fields, W.C. 34, 44
Fishponds mental hospital 16,
    35
Fisk, Jim 43
Fontaine, Joan 73-4, *74-5*, 76,
    81
Foreman, Carl 128
Forester, C.S. 128
Fox, *see* Twentieth Century Fox
Francis, Kay 56
Frank, Melvin 109
Friedlander, William 21
Front Page, The 29, 57, 60
Furthman, Jules 55

Gable, Clark 36, 111
Gallico, Paul 42
Gambling Ship 32
Garbo, Greta 23, 52
Garland, Judy 56, 121
Gering, Marion 21
Gibney, Sheridan 81
Gill, Brendan 160
Goetz, Kurt 116
Golden Dawn 16, 19
Goldwyn, Sam 104
Gone with the Wind 63, 73
Good Times 17-18
Gordon, Ruth 103
Grady, Billy 21
Graham, Sheilah 164
Grand Hotel 173
Grandon Productions 138
Grant, Barbara, *see* Harris, B.
Grant, Cary:
    accent 18-19, 187
    acrobatic skills 17
    acting ability 62, 67, 84

acting ambitions 15-17, 18
American citizenship 54, 56,
    79-80, 82
as Archie Leach 13-23
awards 171, 185, *186*
as businessman 169-71, 175
change of name 20, 21, 23,
    82
character 16, 37-8, 48, 71,
    74, 86, 103, 121-2, 156,
    160, 175
childhood 14-16, *14*
cinema-going 15
and comedy 18-19, 47-8, 50,
    60, 65, 79, 111
death 186
divorces 38, 93-4, 142, 155,
    168-9
drug-taking 145-6, 155, 169
earnings 18, 19, 21, 27, 31,
    32, 38, 42, 53, 61, 79,
    86, 103, 104, 111, 116,
    136, 142, 146, 153, 155,
    168
emotional relationships 32-4,
    44, 57, 60, 62-3, 71-2,
    76, 107, 112, 129-31,
    133-4, 150, *151*, 155,
    159, 175-7, *176*, 180-2
family background 13-16,
    34-5, 177
and fatherhood 72, 162-9,
    171, 173-5, 177
first film role 21
friendships 21, 27, 41, 60,
    88, 104, 121, 136, 142,
    169, 182
goodwill tours 86, *86*
homes 27-9, *28*, 35, 41-2,
    84, 91, 182
illness 112, 186
image 32, 142, 155
investments 27, 53, 142, 175
lecture series 186
marriages 35, 37, 71, 80, 82,
    88, *88*, 90-1, 115, 162,
    162, 182-3
misogynist 48, 175
musical-comedy star *12*, 16,
    19-21
obituaries 187
psychotherapy 145-6, 155
retirement 119, 121-2, 166,
    171, 173, 178
reviews 24, 25, 27, 29, 31-2,
    34, 36, 38, 41, 42, 43,
    44, 49, 51-2, 55, 57,
    60-1, 62, 64, 67, 72, 76,
    81, 82, 86, 88, 89, 90-1,
    94, 99, 103, 104, 110-11,
    112, 116, 117, 119, 126,
    130, 132, 133, 138-41,
    142, 146, 150, 153-5,
    158, 160, 165
schooldays 15-16
screen persona 16, 43, *46*,
    49, 50-2, 55, 56, 69,
    99-101, 131, 141, *142*,
    150-1, 153, 156, 187,
    188
screen tests 20, 21
star status 53, 54, 70, 111,
    122, 130, *141*, 155
stilt-walking 18
studio contracts 23, 42-3, 63
temper 37, 168-9
tributes to 186-7
vaudeville years 17-19, 49
Grant, Jennifer 165-9, *166-7*,
    171, 173-5, *173*, 177, *178-9*,
    180-2, *183-5*, 188
Grass Is Greener, The 149-50,
    150, 175

Greene, Graham 38, 57
Greenwich Village 18, 20
Guinness, Alec 128
Gunga Din 13, 53-4, *53*, *55*,
    72
Gwenn, Edmund 39

Hammerstein, Arthur 19, 20
Hammerstein, Oscar 19
Hammerstein, Reggie 19
Harareet, Haya 150
Hardy, Oliver 47
Harlow, Jean 22, 42, 44
Harris, Barbara *172*, 180-6,
    181-3, *187*, 188
Harrison, Rex 149, 159
Hart, Moss 76, 121
Hartman, Don 110
Hartman, Dr Mortimer 145,
    155
Hawks, Howard 50-1, 53-5,
    57, 59-60, *60*, 74, 81,
    111-12, *112*,
    118, 119, 182
Hawks, Slim 141
Hayes, John Michael 126
Hayworth, Rita 55, *56*
Hearst, William Randolph 37,
    44
Hecht, Ben 53, 57, 97, 118
Hell's Angels 27
Hepburn, Audrey *155-7*,
    156-60
Hepburn, Katharine 39, *40-1*,
    47, 50-2, *51-2*, 54, 64-9,
    68-9, 81
Here Comes Mr Jordan 177
Hippodrome, Bristol 16-17
Hippodrome, New York 17, 18
His Girl Friday 13, 57-60,
    58-60, 65, 67, 111
Hitchcock, Alfred 73-4, *73*, 76,
    96-7, 97-9, 103, 122-5, *123*,
    138, 141-2, *142*, 146, 182
Hodgins, Eric 109
Holden, William 128
Holiday 52-3, *52*, 54, *54*, 64
Hollywood 21, 27
Hollywood Park 175, *176*, 180,
    186
Hollywood Reporter 67, 76,
    90, 117, 119, 142, 160
Hollywood Spectator 42
Holmes, Ernest 122
Holmes, Milton 84
Hope, Bob 79
Hopper, Hedda 71, 86
Hopwood, Avery 24
Hot Saturday 29, *29*
Houseboat 133-4, *134-5*, 142
Houston, John 128
Howards of Virginia, The 63-4,
    63-4
Hughes, Howard 27-9, 38-9,
    44, 50, 59, 62, 64, 111,
    112-15, 116, 182
Hull, Josephine 79
Humbert, George *44-5*
Hume, Benita 32
Hunter, Louise 19
Hussey, Ruth 69
Huston, John 115
Hutton, Barbara 63, 71-2, *71*,
    76, 80, 82, 84-6, 88, *88*,
    90-1, 93-4, 142
Hutton, Jim 163-4, *163*
Hyams, Joe 146

I Was a Male War Bride
    111-12, *112-13*
Iles, Frances 73
I'm No Angel 32, *33*
In Name Only 56-7, *57*

Indiscreet 136-7, 138, 139-41, 149

Jamaica 160
John Hopkins Hospital 112
Johnson, Mabel 34

Kael, Pauline 60, 69, 158, 175
Kanin, Garson 49, 61-2, 103
Karloff, Boris 23
Kaufman, George 76
Keeler, Ruby 37
Keith, B.F. 18
Kelly, Grace 122-6, *123, 126-7,* 141, 156, 183, 185, *185*
Kelly, Jack 18
Kendall, Kay 149
Kennedy Centre 185
Kerr, Deborah 119, *119,* 131-2, *131,* 149-50, *150,* 188
Kesselring, Joseph 76
King Kong 21
Kingdon, Elsie, *see* Leach, E.
Kipling, Rudyard 53
Kiss and Make Up 36, *36*
Kiss Them for Me 133, *133*
Koster, Henry 104
Kovack, Nancy 150
Kramer, Stanley 128
Krasna, Norman 136, 138

Ladd, Alan 130
Ladies Should Listen 36
Landi, Elissa 37
Lane, Priscilla 79
Langdon, Harry 47
Lardner, Ring 159
Last Outpost, The 38
Laughton, Charles 25, *25,* 36
Laurel, Stan 47
Leach, Archibald, *see* Grant, Cary
Leach, Elias 13-17, 34-5, 41, 42, 177
Leach, Elsie 13-16, *15,* 34-5, 41, *54,* 56, 101, 104, 116, 134, 149, 158, 162, 165-6, 177
Leach, John 13-14
Lean, David 128
Lederer, Charles 111, 118
Lehman, Ernest 141
Letter to Three Wives, A 116
Levitt, Alfred Lewis 119
Life 94
Llewellyn, Richard 88
Lloyd, Frank 64
Lombard, Carole 24, *24,* 27, 56, *57*
Lone Pine 54
Lonsdale, Frederick 104
Loren, Sophia 121, 128-31, *128-30,* 133-6, *134-5,* 141, 188
Lorre, Peter 79
Los Angeles County Museum of Art 188
Los Angeles Mirror 116
Los Angeles Times 132, 165, 187
Love Affair 131-2
Love Parade, The 20
Loy, Myrna 37-8, 101-3, *108-9,* 109
Lupino, Ida 90
Lux Radio Theatre 56, 112

MacArthur, Charles 53, 57
McCary, Leo 44, 47-52, 56, 61-2, 74, 81-4, 131-2, *131,* 138
McCrea, Joel 163
MacDonald, Jeanette 20

Mack, Helen 36
McKendry, Margo *152-3*
Mackenzie, Compton 39
McLaglen, Victor 53, *53*
Magic Castle 183
Man Who Came to Dinner, The 76
Mankiewicz, Joseph L. 64, 67, 116, 173
Mann, Delbert 153
Mansfield, Jayne 131, 133, *133*
March, Fredric 24, 31, *32*
Marx Brothers 47
Massey, Raymond 79, *79*
Mayer, Louis B. 64
Merrill, Dina *151*
Metropole Cinema, Bristol 15
Mexico 76
MGM 20, 31, 36, 42, 44, 52, 63, 64, 115, 119, 142, 159, 173, 175, 178, 185-6
Miller, Marilyn 20
Mr Blandings Builds His Dream House 108-10, 109-10, 116
Mr Lucky 84-6, *84-5*
Mitchum, Robert 149, 188
Monkey Business 118, *118*
Monroe, Marilyn 118-19, *118*
Monte Carlo 141
Moore, Grace 43
More the Merrier, The 163
Moreno, Antonio 115
Moscow 141
Mountbatten, Lord 182
Music Man, The 151
Mutiny on the Bounty 36, 42
My Fair Lady 158, 160
My Favorite Wife 61-2, *61,* 62

Nathan, Robert 104
Nation 54, 60, 89
Navarro, Ramon 115
Neale 27
Nelson, Nancy 186
Nelson, Ralph 160
New Republic 49, 72
New York 17-18, 19, 21, 41, 168
New York Herald Tribune 90
New York Times 27, 34, 36, 41, 44, 49, 51-2, 60, 62, 64, 67, 82, 88, 90, 99, 104, 112, 116, 119, 126, 133, 136, 150, 158, 160, 187
New Yorker 76, 110, 119, 132, 158, 160, 165
Newsweek 55, 64, 81, 82, 86, 88, 110, 112, 116, 119, 141, 146, 158, 165
Night and Day 93-4, *93, 94-5,* 187
Nikki 21, 23, 187
Niven, David 104, *105,* 128
None But the Lonely Heart 88-90, *89-91,* 91
Normandie 63
North by Northwest 140-3, 141-2, 168
Norton Simon Museum 180
Norwich 17
Notorious 92, 97-101, *99-101,* 136
Novak, Kim *151*

Oakie, Jack 34, 43
O'Brien, Joan *147*
Odets, Clifford 88-90, *89,* 141
Once Upon a Honeymoon 56, 61, 81-2, *83*
Once Upon a Time 87-9

Only Angels Have Wings 54-6, *55-6,* 59
Operation Petticoat 144-5, 145-6, *147,* 175
Orry-Kelly 18
Our Town 63

Pacific Palisades 84, 90, 91
Page, Elizabeth 63
Paglia, Camille 188
Palace Theatre, Broadway 18
Palm Springs 115, 122, 128, 183
Panama, Norman 109
Pantages, Alexander 18
Paramount 20-38, 42, 47, 125, 134, 156
Paramount decree 118
Parker, Dorothy 121
Parker, Suzy 133, *133*
Parsons, Louella 30, 32, 41, 90, 91, 112, 134, 150
'Pass Me By' 160
Pender, Bob 17-18
Pender, Tommy 18
Pender's Knockabout Comedians 17-18
Penny Serenade 72, *72,* 80, 81
People 187
People Will Talk 116
Perelman, S.J. 126
Philadelphia Story, The 64-9, *65-9,* 71, 81
Photoplay 23, 25, 71, 86
Pidgeon, Walter 42
Poe, James 126
Polly 19-20
Ponti, Carlo 130, 134-6
Porter, Cole 93, 177
Potter, H.C. (Hank) 84, 109
Pride and the Passion, The 128-30, *128-9,* 132, 134
Princess Grace Foundation 187
Pringles Picture Palace, Bristol 15

Radio City Music Hall 41, 99, 150, 155, 158, 160
Rainer, Louise 88
Rainier, Prince 128, 141, 183
Rains, Claude 38
Randall, Tony 131
Reagan, Ronald 185, 186, 187
Rebecca 73
Reventlow, Count 63, 71, 76, 90
Reventlow, Lance 71, 72, 84, 88, 90, 94
Reynolds, Burt 173
Riches and Romance 43
Richlin, Maurice 145
Richman, Arthur 47
Riskin, Robert 43
RKO 39, 42, 43, 50-4, 56, 61-2, 73, 76, 81, 82, 84, 88-9, 94-5, 101, 104, 107-10, 111
Roach, Hal 44
Robson, May 51
Rochard, Henri 111
Rodann, Ziva 150
Rogers, Ginger 44, 56, 61, 81, *83,* 118, *118*
Roland, Gilbert 115
Room for One More 116-18, 117
Rosalie 20
Rose, Anna Perrott 117
Rose, Jack 117, 133-4
Rossellini, Roberto 136, 138
Russell, Rosalind *58-60,* 59-60, 82, 182
Ryskind, Morrie 72

Sabrina 156
Saint, Eva Marie *140-1,* 141-2, 187
St John, Adela Rogers 121
St Louis Municipal Opera 21
Saks, Sol 163
Sanders, George 116
Santa Monica 42, 44, 84, 168
Saturday Evening Post 90
Saunders, John Monk 21, 23, 31
Scarface 29, 50
Schary, Dore 103, 107-9, 115, 119
Schenk, Joe 42
Schickel, Richard 187
Schulberg, B.P. 21, 23, 25, 29, 32, 36
Scott, Adrian 84
Scott, Martha 63, *64*
Scott, Randolph 27-9, *28, 35, 35,* 41, 53, 60, 61, 82, 88
Segal, George 173
Seiter, William 104
Selznick, David O. 73, 97, 107-9, 116
Sergeant York 81
Shaffer, Anthony 173
Shamus 173
Shanghai Express 25
Shapiro, Stanley 145, 153
Shavelson, Mel 117, 133-4
Shaw, Irwin 80
She Done Him Wrong 30-1, *30-1*
Sheldon, Sidney 101, 103, 119, *119*
Sheridan, Ann 112
Sherman, Lowell 30
Sherman, Richard 56
Sherwood, Robert 104
Shubert, Lee & J.J. 20-1
Sidney, Sylvia 29, 35-6
Siegel, Bugsy 63
Silver Screen 29
Simmons, Jean 149
Sinatra, Frank 128-9, 130, 142, 171, 183, 187
Singapore Sue 13, 17, 21
Sinners in the Sun 24, *24*
Sleepless in Seattle 132
Sleuth 173
Smith, Alexis 93, 187
Smith, Queenie 20
Some Like It Hot 145
Southern, Terry 159
Spectator 38, 57
Spewack, Bella & Samuel 61
Spiegel, Sam 128, 141
Spigelglass, Leonard 111
Star Is Born, A 121
Stark, Ray 107
Stevens, George 53-4, 72, 80, 163
Stewart, Donald Ogden 64, 69
Stewart, James 64-5, *66-7,* 69, 187
Stillman, Patricia 88
Stone, Peter 156, 159-60
Street Singer, The 21
Suspicion 73-6, *73-7,* 81
Suzy 22, 42
Sylvia Scarlett 39-42, *40-1,* 50

Talk of the Town, The 80-1, *80-1*
Talmadge, Norma 42
Tarloff, Frank 160
Taurog, Norman 117
Taylor, Elizabeth 187
Temple, Shirley 101-3, *103,* 112
Tennent, H.M. 107

Thalberg, Irving 36
That Touch of Mink 153-5, *154,* 175
Theatre Royal, Norwich 17
Thin Man, The 37
Thirty Day Princess 35-6
This Is the Night 24, *24*
Thyssen, Greta 155
Tilyou, George 18
Time 41, 52, 57, 62, 90, 94, 110-11, 117, 130, 132, 187
To Catch a Thief 123-6, *123, 125-7,* 156
Toast of New York, The 43, *43*
Todd, Mike 126
Todd, Thelma 24
Tokyo 163-4
Tone, Franchot 36, 42
Topper 44, *44-5*
Touch of Class, A 173
Twentieth Century Fox 112, 116, 118, 131, 133, 151

United Artists 36
Universal 23, 145-6, 151-3, 160, 175

Variety 21, 24, 25, 29, 31-2, 36, 38, 41, 42, 43, 60, 67, 72, 76, 81, 90, 103, 104, 117, 126, 146, 150, 153-5
Vincent, Frank 42, 103
von Sternberg, Josef 25-7, 29

Wakeman, Frederick 133
Walk Don't Run 148, 163-5, *163-5*
Walking Stanleys 18
Walsh, Raoul 42
Walters, Charles 163
War Department 84
Warner, Jack 79, 86, 90, 158
Warner Brothers 76-9, 86-7, 90, 93, 116, 121, 136, 149, 151
Wedding Present 42
Wellman, William 121
Wenke, Judge Robert 169
West, Mae 30-2, *30-1,* 33
What Price Hollywood? 121
When You're in Love 43
Wilde, Hagar 50, 111
Will Success Spoil Rock Hunter? 130
William Morris Agency 21
Williams, Hugh & Margaret 149
Wing, Toby 37
Wings in the Dark 37-8, 38
Woman Accused 31
Wonderful Night, A 20, 21
Woodward, Joanne 168
Woolley, Monty 76
World War I 16
World War II 54, 69, 79, 82, 84, 86
Wray, Fay 21, 187

Young, Loretta 36, 104
Young, Roland 24, 44

Zanuck, Darryl 116
Ziegfeld, Florenz 20
Zukor, Adolph 23, 25, 30, 31, 34, 36, 42, 47